Real Life Stories

Real People

in

Real Places

with

Real Problems

looking for a

Real Answer

People so Real that it could be someone that you know.

Table of Contents

Additional Table of Contents

CHAPTER 1

Vietnam Almost Destroyed Me

Vietnam almost destroyed me. After 28 years of drug and alcohol abuse, I found freedom. I was brought up in a nice home, but left at the age of 15. I was introduced to the world of drugs and alcohol when I was very young. It was the beginning of a turmoil that would follow me for a long time.

Years later, I found myself on foreign soil. I was in the army and fighting in a war that didn't make sense to me. When I returned home from Vietnam, I was a very disturbed man. Like many veterans of that war, I was a ball of confusion.

I married a wonderful woman, but my drug use and destructive ways continued. My wife and I had four beautiful children, but I still continued in my awful ways. I failed in many areas in my parental and marital responsibilities. My wife endured many years of verbal abuse, due to the drugs and alcohol I thought I could never give up.

I started attending church with my wife and children, who continually prayed for me. Sometimes my wife's prayers at home were so intense that she would start speaking in tongues, and I would have to run out of the house to get away from it. Many times the Lord spoke to me, but I didn't want to listen.

I remember at one time being so messed up on drugs, that I finally called on the pastor of my wife's church to pray for me. My life was in complete turmoil. I still refused to serve the Lord, but the pastor continued to come over and pray for me. He never lost faith that God would save me, yet my drug use continued. I had tried so many times to quit and had even admitted myself to a hospital for rehabilitation. Nothing worked. But for God, nothing is impossible.

In November of 1993, after 28 years of abusing drugs and alcohol, I was in church asking the Lord to break those chains, as I had done many times before. That day, the pastor started praying for me like he had done many times before, and then two other men from the church were right behind me. As they continued praying, I felt a burning sensation come over my body. It was something I had never felt before. I felt like a heavy load was lifted off my chest. What a glorious day! It has been almost ten years, and I am still alcohol and drug free.

What I put my family through was awful, but I thank the Lord for a wonderful wife, four beautiful children, and for a loving pastor and church family. After such a long rocky road, the Lord saved me and restored my life. There are areas in my life that I still need to change, and with God's help I will succeed.

I pray that sharing my story will help you with any similar circumstances you are going through. If you need a change in your life, God is the answer. The world has nothing to offer but pain and misery. In God, there is hope. What God has done for me, He will do for you. If you have been verbally abusive or hooked on drugs or alcohol, you can change. Believe me, I know. These things had a hold on me for 28 years. Today, thanks to God, I am free. Friend, get free and stay free.

— *Hector*

CHAPTER 2
I Heard The
Doctor Say...

I heard the doctor say, "I have done all I can do for her. Only a miracle will save her." It was my mother the doctor was talking about, and I was just 5 years old. At age 5, I could not imagine not having my mom there with me. I had so many responsibilities, and at only 5 years old, my life was in shambles.

I would often hear my mom praying, and that showed me what I had to do. I went to the corn field and cried out, asking God to heal my mother. With child-like faith, I knew God would hear my prayers. When I got back to the house, my mom began to get better. She was healed.

That was 81 years ago, and it was several years before I got serious with God. I learned that day - there is power in prayer. I married a man years later that was of a different faith. He would remark, "I was born in this faith, and I'll die in it." When our children were grown, they would try to tell him about Jesus, but he did not want to hear any of it.

One day, my husband had to have major surgery. Our youngest son wrote out the plan of salvation one evening, just before visiting hours were over and left it by his bedside. From then on, my husband claimed salvation. He became a dedicated believer and loved working in the church. This was a miracle. He has since gone on to be with the Lord.

I have three children serving God, several grandchildren in the ministry, and several great-grandchildren in the church. When I go to church, I feel so blessed to be surrounded by all my loved ones. God is so good. He has blessed me with good health. I am now 86 years of age. Aches, pains and sleeping problems are part of my life now, but God sees me through everything. Sometimes I get lonely, and then God reminds me of the corn field, how He still hears my prayers, and how He is still my

Heavenly Father. He cares for me like no other. He is leaving me here on earth for a reason. I can still pray, and my faith is as strong as it was 81 years ago. God has done so much for me over the years. I feel Him every day. So can you if only you believe and accept Christ into your heart. He will never leave you. My prayer for you is that you will be blessed and that you will turn your eyes to Jesus and let Him bless you with a long and healthy life.

You do not have to go into a corn field to cry out to God. You can do it right now, right where you are. God is listening for you and wants to help you.

— *Marie*

CHAPTER 3

Arrested for Attempted Murder!

Arrested for ATTEMPTED MURDER! Alcohol, Drugs, Anger, and Rage took me to a place I never wanted to go…

I started doing drugs while in high school. An older brother turned me on to marijuana. I was having an identity crisis, and the drugs seemed to help. I coasted thru my classes and graduated. Then I went to college. It was there that I discovered I could sell this to other kids and make money!

It was also there that I discovered the bad side of drugs. During the Easter Holiday, a couple of us stayed in the dorm. The Dean caught us in full party mode with beer, wine, and reefer!

I decided to come home and go to I.U. Indiana University told me that due to my incomplete semester, I would just be an advanced freshman. I said no way and went to work in the mills, selling marijuana to supplement my income.

Another brother and I were renting out the basement apartment in my parents' home. One day, one of our drug customers couldn't find us, so he asked my mom if she had any weed to sell! After that, some guys came and robbed us at gun point. I knew then I had to get that kind of lifestyle away from my parents. It was the Holy Spirit convicting me then!

Later on that year, I got hired at the Post Office. God was making a way for me to get out of that lifestyle. The security of a steady job, and a constant tugging at my spirit to be righteous, helped me to stop dealing. I was still using though. I tried cocaine and liked it. Then I started smoking it. Big trouble.

I met a "coke-man" who would front me any amount I wanted. I was still working, but I was working for my habit. Bills went unpaid, and my temper was flaring. I was a mess.

It was around this time that I met my wife. We dated, then got married, and then divorced. She went through all these things that I did. Once, while trying to get back together, we went out—drinking, drugging, and arguing. The argument got out of hand, and her sister's husband got out of the car. They had been arguing too. He said he would walk home, so she told me to get out too. Then he took off in a rage. I got out and couldn't find him, so I was by myself. By this time, I was in a rage! I got a couple of rides to the state line. I was really wet and furious. When I got back to Gary to her house, I made a very foolish move. I let the rage in me build and I hit my wife in the head with a sledge hammer. I knew instantly that I was wrong. I took her to the hospital. Her dad pulled a gun on me, and told me to get out of there.

When I first went to jail, the Lord instructed me to read His word. I know this is what everyone does when they first go to jail, "Jailhouse Religion". But this was different. God told me that He would take care of me. I felt that I was completely unworthy of His loving kindness! He provided a jailer for me that was from my neighborhood. This jailer watched over me, uplifted me, and told me that he knew I was a good person. At this time, I definitely did not feel like a "good person!"

My wife was in the hospital, in critical condition. My two sons were without a mom and dad. I felt like I was losing everything. When I got out, I vowed that I would set things straight. While sitting at home, unable to go to work, unable to go see my wife, and unable to see my kids; the Lord sent a saint by. This young man knocked at my door. I looked out and saw a young white boy. I knew he was a "Bible Thumper." Normally I would just ignore these guys and they would go away. This time the Lord had made me ready. This young man was out being obedient, trying to save souls! He asked me if I knew Christ as my savior.

I told him he should run from me, and that I was that awful man who had almost killed his wife. He said that Jesus loved me and would forgive me if I just asked Him to. I surrendered to the Lord and let Him fill me. This young

13

man's sincere prayer and determination won me over.

The Lord already had me reading my Bible while I was off. Things began to change. Vickie's health was improving. (Though at one time, word was that she had passed.) She was slowly coming around each day and getting stronger. One of her family members arranged for me to see my sons! After 3 weeks, Vickie got out. She came to see me. That just broke my heart. Here was this woman that I just hurt so bad standing at my doorway. She told me that she still loved me and forgave me. I felt so unworthy of her love. I vowed that I would never ever fight my wife again. With God's help I have kept that vow since 1986. We reconciled, broke up again, got back together, broke up again, got back together, just going through a cycle. We both got back into drugs, reefer, and coke. Then one day, it just clicked. God had not saved us both just to fall back into sin!

My wife and kids started going to church regularly. I was sitting at home watching football, smoking joints, drinking beer. But I could see the change in her! She quit smoking cigarettes and reefer! She changed her whole lifestyle. I realized she was setting a better example than me. I had gotten everything back, but still felt a void. I had backslidden. I realized that I had better get right with God. He was the one that had saved me, not me! I made up my mind to go to church with my family. Since that time, God has set me free of drugs, drinking and anger.

Friend, if you are dealing with any of the same problems I had, you need help. You can't fix it. Man can't fix it. Only God can help you.

— *David*

CHAPTER 4
I Just Wanted to Feel Accepted

I just wanted to feel accepted, to fit in, to be part of the group. I tried cigarettes to fit in. I tried alcohol to fit in. Today, my life is full and complete, and I fit in perfectly. To find out how, continue...

I grew up in a small town in Pennsylvania. I can always remember being in church. In fact, at age 13, I was saved at church. I liked going to church. I always felt it was the right thing to do. I also liked feeling accepted and being part of a group. I had a good-girl image, and I wanted to live up to that. So being a good-girl meant going to church. The world also had some things to offer. So, if cigarettes meant being popular, I tried cigarettes. If drinking could get me accepted, I tried drinking. There was always that fear of letting someone down. That someone was first of all God, then my family. My father worked in a car factory, and my mother was a housewife. I had an older sister and a younger brother. My father was very strict, so I definitely did not want to get caught. I had an aunt who lived in another town about 12 miles away. My sister and I used to love to stay at her house. My aunt and uncle would let us stay a couple weeks in the summer or the whole summer. They would spoil us and we loved it. The summer I turned 13, I was staying at my aunt's when I met Jim. We liked each other and hung out together over the summer. When school started back up, we broke it off. Two years later, Jim called to invite me to a post-prom picnic. I went, and then we started dating. Dating was difficult because we went to different schools. We saw each other on weekends and when there was no school. Then we made a big mistake. We became sexually active. I remember at first I didn't want to do it. I was so mad at myself when I gave in. I knew I couldn't take it back. We had to sneak around to be together because once we started, we couldn't stop. In 1972 I was 15 years old. My dad had been diagnosed with cancer. On September 23, 1972, my father died of cancer at the age of 41. Jim and I continued to date, and a year later we got engaged. Jim was two years older than me, and in 1973 he graduated from high school. He was enrolled at a computer school in Pittsburgh. He had relatives that lived in Indiana, and they were working at different Steel Mills. They raved about how much money they were making. So, Jim decided to go to Indiana for the summer and make some money. Once he got to Indiana, he liked it, so he decided to stay. After he was out there for awhile, he got homesick and wanted for us to get married sooner. I wanted to finish high school. I had one year left. He asked me to marry him and said I could finish school in Indiana. I was scared. I didn't know what to do. I gave in and said yes. Over the next year, there were a lot of emotions about getting married because I was saved and he was not. Although I had been pretty wishy-washy about being a Christian. Jim found a church in Indiana that would marry us. That was hard, not only because I was saved and he was not, but also because we came from two different faiths. We were married June 22, 1974. Before we got married, I said that I would pray and believe, and that in a short while Jim would be saved. That short while took 19 years! A couple of years after we got married, I got serious about being a Christian. I still wanted to be that good girl and do the right things. I am glad that I never got addicted to the alcohol or the cigarettes. I would smoke and drink on and off to try to fit in, but I always felt guilty. Eventually, with the help of God, I quit smoking and drinking and never went back to it. Jim, on the other hand was a drinker and a smoker. He went out with his friends a lot. Sometimes, he wouldn't come home until 4 or 5 in the morning. We started a family after we were married 7 months. I did go to school here in Indiana, and I graduated. I became focused on the children and continued praying for Jim to get saved. Jim and I had 4 children—1 daughter and 3 sons. I raised them in church. Jim never kept his family from going to church. I praise God for that. At times it was hard, because I didn't think he would ever get saved. I remember once in 1980 when he went out drinking and didn't come home for two days. After that, he quit drinking and smoking. It was amazing, but he still didn't get saved. The church I was attending started standing and agreeing with me for Jim to be saved. There were times when I would get on his case about being saved, and I knew I was just pushing him away. I tried to reach him by my lifestyle. I did that by being the kind of wife and mother that God wanted me to be. That helped me to see that I didn't need to find man's approval any more. I only needed to have God's approval. Finally, on March 21,

16

1993, Jim was saved. Praise God. I do praise God for saving my husband, and for getting me on track. The hardest part of the story is that I committed all of these sins after I was saved. That bothers me so much, especially the premarital sex. I did repent, and I know I was forgiven because I John 1:9 says *"If we confess our sins, He is faithful and just to forgive us our sins, and to cleanse us from all unrighteousness."* I kept feeling guilty until I allowed Jesus to completely set me free. I was forgiven, but Satan tried to convince me that I wasn't. Satan is a liar. Two years after we were married, I was baptized in the Holy Spirit, and it felt like God opened up my head and poured love through me. That really ushered me to a place of wanting to be set apart for God. It was still a process that brought me to where I am today. Life is full and complete with Jesus as my Savior. I do not want to live without Him. It is only because of Him that I am where I am. He is my everything. I love You Jesus. I thank You Jesus. I praise You Jesus.

— *Carla*

17

CHAPTER 5
If Only I Had
Listened to My Parents

If only I had listened to my parents. Yell!!! Scream!! Why??? NO ONE KNEW I WAS THERE!!!!

I was brought up in a home with two parents that loved me deeply. They watched out for me and told me of the people they liked me hanging out with and those they did not care for me to hang out with. (Of course, they were always right). The ones that were "not so good" for me were the ones I was drawn to.

Moms, Dads, Parents, share my true story with your children. Help them to learn by my mistakes. Teach them to obey those in authority over them. Teenagers and young adults, read my story and learn from it. Don't make the mistakes I made. Obey those in authority over you.

I had a friend in my life at the age eight that I trusted, if that is what an eight year old child would think of as friendship. She wanted to go on a so-called journey to her "grandfather's" house. I didn't have a problem with this. All we had to do was go through the forest directly behind my house to get there. It wasn't a far walk, and we wouldn't be gone long so my mother wouldn't worry.

Needless to say, I went where I wasn't supposed to go. I found that the consequences of my actions had a far worse price than I wanted to pay.

The man we went to see was **NOT** my friend's grandfather. He was a child molester, and I was about to be the next child he took advantage of.

Yell??? Scream??? — Why???? NO ONE KNEW I WAS THERE!!!!

I was there, despite what I was told. If only I had listened to my parents. Now, I was faced with the consequences of my actions. Those were some harsh consequences to have to face at eight years old for not listening. You think I would have learned my lesson, but as a teenager, things in my life only seemed to get worse. I made my life worse by thinking it was okay, because I had excuses for the way that I was behaving. The only real stability I knew was from my Mom and Dad, who had been together for 20 years. Then they decided to get a divorce. *How could this happen? Who was to blame? Who could I turn to?* Surely not God. We had all gotten too busy to talk to Him. This day to day life was too much. Too much on me, too much on my Mom and Dad's marriage, and too much on my brother who was now turning to dangerous things to fulfill his life. But, because we kept our heads above water, we thought everything was all right. As a teenage girl, I started dating men I shouldn't have been dating. I started skipping school, I started stealing, I started dressing VERY sexy, I started having sex, and I started drinking. I did all of these things for attention. It was the wrong kind of attention. I got into an abusive relationship, which I made excuses for. I let this kind of trash into my life and chose to deal with it. WHY WOULD A CHILD CHOOSE TO DEAL WITH SOMETHING LIKE THAT??? After awhile, I asked myself the same question. I told myself I would never let a man treat me that way. I would never be this little "mousy" woman. People would hear me, and they would hear me loud and clear. The first thing I did was run. I didn't run to God and ask Him to help me or heal me from the burdens I carried. I ran to a man, a man that I thought would take care of me, a man that I thought would love me despite what anyone thought. He was my brother's best friend. I married him for all the wrong reasons, which I was soon to find out. Our marriage consisted of yelling, screaming, cursing, broken glasses, tipped over entertainment centers, broken doors, and broken windows. You name it, I did it. I blamed him for the way my life was. I went out all the time, I got drunk all the time, and I didn't care what anyone said. I was doing what I wanted to do. I started cheating, and I started lying. I was doing all the things that were ever done to me. So, after only one year of marriage, I filed for a divorce. Happy??? I sure thought I was. I was living on cloud nine. I worked in a place that filled my head with more garbage than one person should ever encounter in their life. I was making great money. I had always thought men were all dogs, and those dogs were now paying my bills. Stupid men, married men!!! Men with degrees, men with more money then they knew

19

what to do with. I didn't care how I was getting it. All I cared about was making it on my own. All I had to do is talk to them and give them a little attention, and they gave it to me like water. Yes, people said, "You don't have any morals to work in a strip club." But who needed morals? I had more money then they did, and I was only 21. TWENTY-ONE YEARS OLD, a drunk, a whore, a fighter, a woman who thought it was okay to treat men like they were a piece of trash, because that is how most men treated women. I was just the revenge on men to most women because I didn't care about them or their feelings. I told them everything they wanted to hear. This went on for many years in my life until one day I woke up and said to myself "When are you going to make things different?" "When are you going to change the patterns in your life?" I couldn't go on living this way because by this time, I had two beautiful children. How could I keep destroying their lives? That's when I went to church, and everything changed. I went to a church I had once known as a teen. It was the church my "first real boyfriend" took me to. Little to my surprise, he was still attending. So was his family, who had at one time opened their hearts and lives to me. Once again, I stepped into church and they all opened their arms to me and were glad to see me. Not only was it good to see that some things never change, it was good to know that someone still had some consistency in their life, after living in this crazy world we live in today. And of course, as always, the pastor was amazing. He seemed to never have a judging bone in his body. He always embraced me with such love and compassion. "How did he do it?" I always asked myself. "How could he just keep giving when it felt like there was nothing more to give?" I found out how. I gave my life to the Lord, and it has been a wonderful, life changing experience. I no longer drink or smoke. I no longer long for men or bars in my life. I long for a deeper love and stronger love no man can ever offer. I long for Jesus Christ and in knowing where I stand with Him. I was able to put my pro-miscuous past behind me. I was able to put away the hurt of being mo-lested. I was able to put away the fear that all men were dogs and out to hurt me. I was able to put it all under the blood of Jesus. Then God sent me someone I'm very thankful for. That someone is my husband and my best friend under God. The "first real boyfriend" I had ever had came back. Not because he thought I was beautiful. He was scared to death of my past—my marriage, my children, EVERYTHING!! God let my husband overlook those things once I was new in Christ. The best thing God has ever done for anyone was to give His ONLY son for us to renew our lives.

It is never too late! I'm still learning and still growing. I still have to listen to people remind me of my past, but I know God has forgotten it. Is it hard to hear? Yes, sometimes it is. But it's not as hard as it was to live it! I would rather hear it or tell it any day than relive it. God has delivered me. He continues to deliver me and continues to bless me. I couldn't be more thankful. I know God is not done with me yet. He has brought me a long way. I'm so thankful to Him for forgiving me for breaking His heart!!

I pray that you too would ask Him to forgive you for breaking His heart. All He has ever wanted for you and for me is happiness. The only way you can get that is through Christ. That void will never be filled unless you give it to Him. I'm 28 years old now, and I've never been happier. Do I still endure trials? Of course I do. I'm human. But how I handle them is different. I don't fight with my fist anymore. I'm learning not to fight with my mouth either. God will fight my battles for me. Now, I have the BOOK OF LIFE as a guide and a pastor that helps me to deal with my questions and problems on a spiritual level, not a fleshly one. Trust me when I say the grass isn't always greener on the other side. The crowd you may be with today may not be the crowd there for you tomorrow.

Remember, Jesus Christ is always there no matter what!! No matter what time, no matter what the circumstance, He will be there.

— *Michelle*

CHAPTER 6
I Heard A
Voice Saying...

I heard a voice saying ... "It's time to stop running away from me and start running to me." I was 13 years old when I felt God calling me to preach, but I said "NO!"

I grew up in a Christian home. My mother had prayed my father to Christ when I was very young. I had always had great examples that lived before me, to show me how to live the Christian life, but I had never really enjoyed that life myself.

I was in Jr. High School when I first felt the need for the Lord myself. So I began my journey to know Jesus. It was when I was 13 that God spoke to me and told me that He wanted me to preach, but there was absolutely no way I was going to do that. I told God, "NO!"

From that day, I was determined to mess myself up so bad that God wouldn't be able to use me. I thought that if I would really garbage my life up, I would be safe from this thing that God wanted me to do. I began by experimenting with drugs. At the age of 13, I started smoking dope and doing anything else I could get my hands on, short of putting anything directly into my veins with a needle. I was hanging out with people who would give me anything that I wanted. It didn't take long for me to begin to feel the need to party all the time, and to party all by myself. They say that one of the signs of being an alcoholic or drug addict was that you didn't have to have anybody to party or drink with. Well, I found out it was just as easy to get high alone as it was to get high with someone else. I had started drinking anything. Beer, wine, whiskey, vodka – mixed or straight, it didn't matter. One afternoon while standing out in front of a friend's house, we heard a gun shot. One of my friends had shot himself while huffing glue. I just kept getting high.

By the time I was a junior in High School, I was smoking three joints with my friends every morning before going to school. I would drive to school, high, because I didn't want to face my teachers straight. I often took downers and speed, dropped acid, it was all the same to me. I became so good at what I was doing that the only time my parents suspected I was high was when I wasn't. I didn't handle being straight very well. I would get extremely irritable.

I started staying out very late. One Saturday night, I never came home at all. And I was so numb to my parents that I didn't care if they worried about me or not. My actions and attitude toward my parents, who had never done anything but love me and care about me, became more and more rebellious. I guess it was my way of hiding what was really going on in my life. When they would try to talk to me, I would only yell and talk to them with absolutely no respect. My life was so messed up.

I had begun to skip going to church. I would make plans to go to church. I would tell my parents I would see them there, and I just wouldn't show up. One Sunday night after blowing off church, I had been partying pretty heavy and picked up a couple of my friends and was headed toward their house when I pulled in front of an oncoming Buick – a big one. My car was destroyed, the State police said we all should have been killed, but we walked away without a scratch. I knew then that someone was watching out for me.

During my senior year in High School, my dad asked me to go to the church that our new Pastor was moving in, and they needed some people to help. So I went. It would be the turning point in my life. This guy was young, and he didn't try to judge me. He just had compassion for me. He reached out that day and the days to follow. He could see the junk in my life. One Sunday night, I decided to go to church. Everything was messed up. My friends had started ignoring me. I thought that I had nothing to lose, but I did. That night as the Pastor preached, and I couldn't tell you what he said, I heard a voice saying, "It's time to stop running away from me, and start running to me." I couldn't even contain myself. I thought that I was hearing voices I would only hear when I was on Acid, but it was the voice of God. He said, "No matter what you do, I'll still love you." I got out of my seat, ran to the altar, and asked Jesus to help me. I told Him I would do whatever He wanted if He would only take this hunger for drugs out of my life. He did! That was October 12, 1975. I have been clean since that day.

I prayed to the Lord that night and told Him I would do anything, but when He said, "I don't repent of my call, you already know what I want you to do." I said, "Lord, how could you use me, as dirty and junky as I have made my life." He said, "But you're not dirty anymore. I have made you clean. You are forgiven!" I learned that day, that no matter how bad your life begins, it's how it ends that really matters with the Lord.

My friend, if you are dealing with unforgiveness, especially of yourself, I know that God can forgive. If you are struggling in your life with drugs and alcohol, I know that Jesus Christ can make you free. The Bible declares, "And you shall know the truth, and the truth shall make you free... Therefore if the Son makes you free, you shall be free indeed." (John 8:31,36 NKJV) I am free, and you can be too.

— *Bill*

24

CHAPTER 7
As I Raised A Knife To My Throat...

As I raised a knife to my throat... I heard something that changed my life forever. "I love you. I have a plan for you."

I stood in my mothers' kitchen with a butcher knife to my throat, ready to plunge it through my neck. I was depressed, angry, afraid, and hurt. I felt worthless and useless, just like the trash that needed to be taken out. I had been beaten, taunted, ridiculed, shamed, and molested. I had been rejected and felt unloved. Before I had completed my plan, God began His. I heard His voice. "I love you. I have a plan for you."

I stopped and chose to search for who it was that loved me. I began to have a relationship with God, unique to me. I never knew the depth of this type of love. All I knew was that God loved me and He had a plan for me. Salvation. Life with God. Choosing His way (to live) instead of my way (to die). He has carried me through. God has healed me, delivered me, and made me whole.

He has a plan for you as well. Choose Christ. Give all your hurts and sorrows to Him today.

– *Beth*

The Truth

The people you have just read about had to come to a place of knowing, understanding, and accepting the truth before their lives could be changed.

Throughout the rest of this book, in between the many more "Real Life Stories," we will share some of these truths with you.

God's Law

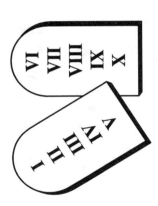

THE TEN COMMANDMENTS

1. You shall have no other gods before me

2. You shall not make yourself any graven image

3. You shall not take the Name of the Lord your God in vain

4. Remember the Sabbath Day to keep it holy

5. Honor your father and mother

6. You shall not kill

7. You shall not commit adultery

8. You shall not steal

9. You shall not lie

10. You shall not covet

Each of the people you have read about had to face God's Law.

Have You Obeyed God's Law?

Are You Sure?

You can go to the next page and read several more "Real Life Stories" or you can skip ahead to our next truth on page 44.

CHAPTER 8
My Marriage Was Dead

My marriage was dead and I was in the basement of my home contemplating suicide.

I have been at Jubilee Worship Center for about 25 years. When I first came to visit this church, I was a broken woman. I had been in church for many years, but I had no peace or joy, nor the abundant life that God promises in His word. I don't think that I ever prayed or read the Word like I was supposed to. I didn't have a relationship with the Lord Jesus Christ. I was very faithful to bring my four children to church, and I paid my tithes. My home life was a living hell. My husband was hooked on drugs and alcohol. He was a very violent man. I was emotionally abused by him. This lifestyle continued for the first 20 years of my marriage. I would come to church faithfully, but something was missing.

It came to the point in my life that I didn't want to live. I thought, "If this is what serving God does for you, I don't want it anymore." I would come home from church and argue and fight with my husband all the time. I lost the love I once had for my husband. I wanted out of the marriage, but in the back of my head I knew that God was not pleased with divorce.

His Word says, *"I can do all things through Christ who strengthens me." Philippians 4:13.* I realized then that something had to be wrong in my life if God was not changing things for me.

As I was in the basement of my home contemplating suicide, I received a telephone call from a sister in the Lord. She told me to pray and seek God because what I was about to do was not the answer to the problem. I took her advice. For six months, all I did was pray and seek an answer from God. One day as I was in prayer, God touched my life. I have

28

never been the same again. God healed my broken heart, my emotions, and my relationship with my husband. I saw my husband in a different way. I started to pray and intercede for him. God delivered him from the drugs and alcohol. He is now serving the Lord with me. There is peace in my home. God has put a song in my heart. He has blessed me abundantly. Now, I understand what it means to be blessed by God. I have everything that my heart desires. My children are also serving the Lord and being healed too. I can say that I love my husband more than I ever did. He is a wonderful man. Praise God I am a free, happy, and fulfilled woman today.

— *Elsie*

CHAPTER 9
Four Fingers Cut Off
In An Accident

Four fingers cut off in an accident. The man picked up the four fingers, held them in place, and cried out.

I was raised in a Christian home. I've never had the desire to experience worldly things. I thank God for the opportunity that He gave me to be born into a Christian home. I can't thank Him enough for that. I have experienced many healings in my body. My God heals minds, hearts, and bodies.

My oldest brother recently refreshed my memory on a healing miracle that my dad experienced. Mom and Dad had ten children, so it was pretty hard to keep track of all of us. One day, my dad was sitting in a church pew listening to a man talk about how he was healed. He was at work, and a piece of heavy machinery took off four of his fingers. The man proceeded to say that he picked up those four fingers, put them in their place, and cried out to God, saying, "God, You know that I need this hand to support my family. Please make my hand whole again!" God performed that miracle, and his hand was healed instantly.

My dad sat there and said, "Yeah, right!" He didn't believe him.

Time went by, and one day my dad was at a small convenience store on 12th Street in Gary. At the same time, my older brother and my younger two-year old brother were walking to the same store. As my brothers crossed the street, my younger brother was hit by a car. The ambulance came and took him to the hospital. While my dad was still in the convenience store, a customer walked into the store and told everyone there that a car had just killed a little boy. My dad said, "Oh my. How much his parents must be suffering."

When my dad finally got home, he saw lots of friends and relatives at our house. They told my dad that his son was hit by a car on his way to the convenience store on 12th Street and was in critical condition in the hospital. My dad didn't believe them. He said, "I know my son is dead." When he arrived at the hospital, the doctor told my dad that his son was in critical condition and that only a miracle could save him.

My dad went home around 9:30pm. When he got home, he dropped to his knees. He cried out before God and said, "Lord, save my son!!!" God showed my dad the hand that He had healed and God asked, "Do you remember this hand? Well, the God that saved that hand is the God that can save your son."

My dad cried out, "I want him healed, Lord!" God then showed that same hand, that my dad once didn't believe, on my brother's head healing the wound.

My brother's recovery was so rapid. The doctor told my dad the very next day that at 10:00 pm, his vital signs had all gone back to normal and that right now his son was sitting up eating his breakfast.

What a mighty God! My God can and will do anything! My God is a healer, a provider, a mender of hearts, and a miracle working God. Please take all your troubles to Him. Only He has all the answers. My friend, if you need a healer, a provider, a heart mender, or a miracle worker, Jesus Christ can be all of these things to you.

— *Dialy*

CHAPTER 10

Loneliness, Anger, & Depression Consumed Me

Loneliness, anger, & depression consumed me. I cried all the time... Then, my life changed completely. For the first time in my life, I felt free...

Since I was a little girl, I remember having this feeling of loneliness. A friend of my mother took care of me because my stepfather and my mother worked. I didn't grow up with siblings or any other relatives.

When my mother died of cancer, I decided to come to the United States. I lived in Rochester, New York with a lady that was related to my future husband. Even though I began a new life, I still had the same feelings of loneliness.

I got married, and within four years, we had three children. We lived in an apartment, and my husband often came home late. I didn't know how to drive, and I didn't have any close friends. I was by myself most of the time. Anger and depression took over my life. I cried all the time, and I just wanted to die. I would ask God why He took my mother and why I always had those awful feelings of loneliness, depression, and anger.

Finally, we decided to move to Indiana to be closer to my husband's family. I started going to my in-laws' church. For the next 20 years, I visited that church. I never became a member, and I never went to the altar.

Then I met Sister Elsie. Within a few years, we started going to college and graduated with degrees in education. For five years, Sister Elsie invited me to go to her church, Jubilee Worship Center. My response was always that I was already going to another church.

In 1995, Jubilee Worship Center was having a Spanish service. I came to church that night, and I sat between Elsie and her sister. When the preaching started, I knew God was speaking to me. He was telling me to stop feeling sorry for myself and that He didn't want me to be a visitor in His house any more. He wanted me to come and make Him my Lord and Savior. I knew I was going to accept Jesus Christ as my Savior that night.

When the altar call was made, I stood up and was ready to go up to the altar. I held onto the front pew with both hands, and I cried. When I was ready to walk to the altar, I could not move. I felt as if my hands were glued to the front pew. I looked at Sister Elsie and at her sister, but they both had their eyes closed in prayer. The enemy had such a strong hold on me, that I could not talk or move. I looked at the woman playing the piano. She looked at me, and I knew that God told her to come down and get me. She came down and asked me if I wanted to go to the altar. I couldn't answer her, but I nodded my head saying yes. She walked with me to the altar and prayed for me. I was saved that night, and I know God sent this sister in the Lord to take me to the altar. My life completely changed. For the first time in my life, I felt free from all those awful feelings I had always had.

God didn't finish with His blessings that night. At the end of that year, we had a three-day revival. The speaker was Brother Billie Joe. On the second day of the revival, he asked how many people wanted to receive the gift of the Holy Spirit, the gift of speaking in tongues. A lot of people came to the altar, and he prayed for all of us. At the end of the prayer, he asked how many of us had been blessed with the gift of speaking in tongues. I raised my hand but then questioned myself because I did not know if I had really received the gift. Brother Billie Joe prayed for us again.

I went home that night happy but also confused. I still didn't know why I had raised my hand. That night my husband slept in another room because he had to get up early in the morning for work, and he didn't want to wake me up. When I laid down in bed, I was still asking myself the same question, "Why did I raise my hand?" Suddenly, I heard myself speaking in another language. This went on for hours. I realized I had been blessed that night with the gift of speaking in tongues.

I have been saved now for almost eight years, and I am happier than ever. Sometimes those awful feelings try to come back to torment me, but I know different now. I have a weapon to fight back——prayer. God is in control of my life, and anything that I need, my Father in heaven will take care of. I also have a second family now, my church family.

Thank You, Jesus, for saving me.

— *Eva*

CHAPTER 11

I Was Hooked On Drugs And Alcohol.

I was hooked on drugs and alcohol. I'd had enough and asked my brother to watch my son while I went into rehab. He said you do not need rehab, you need...

At about 13 years old, I accepted Christ into my life. I was very lonely and just beginning my teen years. I served the Lord for about three years as a bass guitar player in a church band that traveled to other churches, singing contemporary songs. I got mixed up with the wrong crowd near my home and started smoking and drinking at a pretty young age. My parents smoked and drank. During my older teen years, I started trying different drugs. Before I entered into the Air Force, I was drinking regularly and smoking pot. That lifestyle led me to the wrong type of people in the service. I continued to grow further from the Lord and further into drugs and bad relationships. Every once in awhile things would get tough and I would go to church for a couple of weeks and try to be real with God. It never lasted very long.

After having three children and two different wives, my life was going downhill pretty fast. My first child was a severely handicapped boy, Sammy. Just before Sammy was born, I spent some time in the Military jail and in a rehabilitation program. During this time, I again started praying and looking hard for God. Still to no avail. The deeper I got into drugs and alcohol, the harder it was to pray. By this time, I was running cocaine and some other drugs recreationally. I was drinking beer constantly. Along with drugs and alcohol was adultery on both sides. I always had good paying jobs. I was dedicated to them and spent little time with my family. At age 30, I decided it was time to quit drinking and doing drugs, and I moved back to Indiana. For five years, I tried everything to quit. I even went to church occasionally but failed miserably. I just seemed to get deeper into the drug scene. I started smoking crack cocaine. Once I went to Cabrini Green to get some crack. I had a gun in my lap, just in case. After my friend went in to get the crack, a man approached me with one hand stuck in the back of his pants. I knew what that meant. Just as he started getting irate at the fact that I had no business being there, my friend walked out and calmed the man down. At that time I had my gun pointing right at him, where he could not see it. I had every intention of using it if necessary. About three months later, I'd had enough. I told my wife that I was giving up drinking and doing drugs. I told her if she planned to follow me, she needed to do the same thing. She had no intentions of quitting, and she left me. That is when my whole world had finally fallen completely apart. For the first time, I was without my two girls in my life and very lonely. I went to my brother's house and asked him if he would take care of Sammy while I entered into a drug and alcohol rehabilitation. He told me I didn't need to go to rehab. I said he didn't understand where I was at in my life. He said yes he did, and all I had to do was pray and ask God to forgive me and to come back into my life. So I prayed and asked for forgiveness and for God to come back into my life. He forgave me and came back into my life. It has been a tough 10 years since then. I still struggle with many things, but God has never left my side since that day.

Friend, if you are experiencing any of the same problems I went through, only God can help you. He wants to help you, and He is just waiting for you to ask.

— *Mark*

CHAPTER 12
Flirting Led
To Adultery

Flirting led to adultery. Adultery led to divorce. Divorce led to separation. I was separated from my husband and from my Father in Heaven. Separation from God led to repenting, and repenting led to forgiveness.

Today, I'm not proud of my past decisions, but I am happy and thankful that I am totally 100% forgiven. Here's my story:

I grew up in church and was saved when I was about 11 years of age. I wasn't too sure of what that meant. I had parents that brought me to church twice on Sunday and again on Wednesday. I would see my dad sit at the kitchen table praying and reading his Bible, but I didn't know that I should be doing the same.

As I grew up, I did things of this world. I remember one time going to a school football game drunk, and I was promiscuous. My last year of high school I worked two jobs. One was during the week, and the other was on the weekends in Joliet, Illinois. After graduating, I went to work in Joliet full time. This is where I met my future husband. After we were married, things were going pretty good. We had a few arguments like any couple, mostly over money. A few years later, I began to feel like my husband didn't love me anymore. It didn't matter how many times he told me he loved me; I didn't feel loved. I worked outside of the house, and one day I started noticing a man flirting with me. I started thinking this man must notice things about me that my husband didn't. One day, I found myself flirting back with this man, and sometime later I found myself committing adultery with him. I had tried several times to go back to my husband and make things work out, but I always felt out of place.

When I would be at home with my husband, it never felt like it was my home anymore. Things were different. This went on for about six months before I found out that I was pregnant with my first son. Through this whole thing, I knew I was doing wrong. One and a half years later, we were divorced.

Since then, I have had another son, moved back in with my mom and started going to church again. It wasn't until two or three years ago that I asked the Lord to forgive me for breaking one of His commandments. I am now forgiven, living my life for God, and raising my children in church.

Friend, sin can appear very innocent and harmless. Sin will lie to you. Sin will temporarily make you feel better about yourself. Sin will cause you to do things you can not fix, no matter how hard you try. Sin will cause you to do things that you know are wrong. If you have fallen into a life of sin, I hope my story will show you that there is hope, and that you can break free from sin. You can become a new person, and you can be forgiven. Forgiveness starts by asking.

— *Deanna*

CHAPTER 13
I Felt Like I Never Really Fit In

I felt like I never really fit in. I had a difficult time socially and never fit into any group. *Until...*

All my life, I have been raised in church. I have always been in a church atmosphere and heard all the stories. I believe that is why I so easily took for granted the things that should have been so important in my life. My testimony doesn't really start until around the age of 14. Until then, I never buckled against the norm, and I never really made any important decisions in my life.

I was the type of person that had a difficult time socially. I have always felt like I never really fit in with any group of people. I think that is because I have always been one to care very much of how people thought of me. As much as I would try to hide that and bottle it away, it always seemed to surface. Negative thoughts of myself and others would often enter my mind. To me, those in my church seemed to never really want me around, and I could never seem to catch their attention. I began to disconnect myself from church. I was forced to attend church every Sunday, but it was apparent that I wanted nothing to do with it.

I began to find comfort in my less than perfect friends whom I had met over the years. They introduced me to things that I thought would finally bring that sense of acceptance to my life, which I wanted very much. I took up drinking alcohol as something to pass the time with friends. It was exciting and new. I thought that I had found something great, but not even that made me happy. So, I continued to look. I had a friend who was involved in witchcraft and other things of that nature. He wanted me to join him so that he would have a partner in his practice. I thought, "Hey, why not? It looks way more interesting than Christianity."

So, I began living two lives: one of a normal kid not interested in church, and one of a teen into alcohol and witchcraft. Time went on, and I only seemed to fail more and more in my life. Nothing at all seem to be working. Eventually I had enough, and I quit all of the drinking and stopped being a warlock.

I was completely depressed, and I was losing my grip on life. I thought to myself, "So here I am again, empty inside and looking for something to fill the void." Before I had a chance to make another mistake, God sent me an invitation back to Him.

Like a lot of teenage boys, I was very interested in music. I owned a guitar, and the youth group at my church was wanting to start a praise and worship band. I don't know how they knew, but they knew I had a guitar and plucked around on it. The person in charge of the band invited me to be a part of the team. It wasn't my kind of music, but I had always wanted to play in a band. Someone had gone out of their way to invite me to be a part of something, and that meant a lot to me. At first I went in with the mind set that I was just going to use this to gain experience on my instrument. I knew how these church kids were, and I had given them their chance. However, something was different this time.

It was then that I realized that I hadn't been listening to my heart and was running from the things that could save my life. I finally understood that the only thing that was going to make my life better wasn't the people at church, and it wasn't friends with bad habits. It was Jesus Christ, that person I had heard so many stories about. When I let Him into my heart, things became clearer, and I understood what I was missing in my life.

All my life, and as far back as I can remember, I have been raised in church. I knew all the stories, songs, routines, and I thought that I knew what being a Christian was all about. I was wrong! Being a Christian means accepting Jesus Christ into your heart and letting Him fill you up with a love so great, that I can't explain it on paper. My life still gets hard and confusing, but now Jesus gives me a steady foundation to fall back on. That is what everything else the world has to offer is missing.

Friend, let me introduce you to my best friend today. He is waiting to help you today. His name is Jesus. He is the son of God. He loves you.

— *Andrew*

CHAPTER 14
I Was Scared
To Death

I was scared to death. I felt so alone. There was no money coming in, and I could not work. What was I going to do?

I was eighteen when I got married. My thoughts were like a fairy tale; once married always married, until the day you die. My marriage lasted for 10 years, and at the end, I knew it was falling apart. I watched many things happen before my eyes, and there was nothing I could do about it.

I believed in Christ and was married to a non-believer. He said, "If there is a God, let Him come down and show Himself to me." I went to church every Sunday with my child. I was trying everything I knew, but when the time came, he said he was going to leave me. I was pregnant with another child at that time. I had to let him go.

The night he left, I stood at the window looking out and thought, "Here I am with child, a complicated pregnancy, one three year old, and a mighty big world." I was scared to death for all three of us. There was no money coming in, and I couldn't work. What was I going to do?

At that time, I felt very alone. I took one day at a time and continued on. I knew Christ, but I didn't have a close relationship with Him. My God didn't give up on me. When the hard times come along, that's when you find you need God and you talk to Him. I realize now that I would not have made it if God had not carried me through.

My baby was born three months later, a healthy baby boy. Our needs were being met, and I didn't know how. Anger and hurt had to be laid down so that I could get on with my life.

I went to work as a waitress and a cook because it was all I knew. Then I got fired. I wasn't getting any younger and couldn't believe it. I thought I was good at my job. Little did I know, God had something else in store. Doors opened. I went to college and became a medical secretary, and now I have a profession. I could finally work and make an income to take care of my kids and myself.

I am now married to a man of God, who I love very much. I know that God was with me at all times. He'll never forsake you or leave you. The hard times and the good times will always be there, but lean on Him.

Thank you Lord.

— *Cindy*

Sin

On page 27, we asked if you had obeyed God's Law.

Have You?

Most people will say, "Yes, I have, I am a good person." Let's focus now and take a close look at some of God's Laws.

Commandment No. 9 says:

You shall not lie.

Have you ever lied? Told a fib? Maybe just a little white lie? Twisted a story to meet your need? Lied when you were a child? Lied at work? Lied on your tax return? Lied for your spouse or kids?

If I lied, what would that make me? A Liar.

Now let's look at Commandment No. 8.

You shall not steal.

Have you ever stolen? Taken something from work? Taken a piece of candy? Cheated on your taxes? Worked for cash and did not claim it as income? In your younger years, did you take anything that did not belong to you?

What is a person called that has admitted to the above? A Thief.

Now let's look at Commandment No. 7:

You shall not commit adultery.

Have you committed adultery? Jesus said; "Anyone who even looks at a woman with lust in his eye has already committed adultery with her in his heart." Have you every looked at another person with lustful thoughts?

What would a person be called that has done the above? An Adulterer.

At this point we have talked about three of God's Laws. How many have you broken?

Take a moment and go back to page 27 and see if you have broken any more of God's Laws.

From here you can go to the next page and read more "Real Life Stories" or you can skip to page 59 for the next truth.

CHAPTER 15

I Cried...

I Didn't Have A Friend...

I cried... I didn't have a friend... I felt isolated... I was lonely... I was depressed... I drank to feel better... I had money problems... I was consumed with guilt... I was mad... I Just Wanted To Die!

I didn't start out this way. I was raised in a strict Christian home. We had rules the preacher's kids didn't have. I even went to Bible College for a year.

Against my dad's wishes, I married a divorced man with two kids. Nobody from my family would attend the wedding. Later on, they all accepted my husband. We attended church and dedicated our children.

Things began to change when my husband started a band called "*Back-woods*." He soon had little time for me or our children. Weeks would go by when I was alone all the time with the kids. My husband had lots of friends; I didn't have any. I felt isolated.

I started missing church services because my husband wanted me to stay home with him. With his constant traveling, it wasn't hard for me to accept his invitations to come and hear his band play when he was home.

I started drinking one or two drinks to fit in with the crowd I was hanging with. The more popular my husband's band became, the less time he had for me. I was lonely and depressed, so I began drinking to make myself feel better. Before long, I was drinking to get drunk. The mornings after those drunken nights, I would tell my children, "Be real quiet because mommy's head hurts."

We were having money problems, so I got a job as a cocktail waitress at a local bar. Because I had to work until after three in the morning, I was too tired to get up for church. Since I didn't have any church friends, nobody in the church I was attending knew anything about my private life.

I was given free drinks at work, and it is a wonder I never got a DUI on my way home from work. At a family reunion, my sisters told me, "We are praying for you to get your heart right with God." I was so mad! Who did they think they were? What right did they have to judge me! But I couldn't get their words out of my head.

I started having babysitter problems. My children told me of abuses they suffered at the hands of the babysitter while I worked. My guilt consumed me. I quit my job to stay at home with the kids. I decided to get back with God, and I started going to church again.

Two weeks later, my husband's job at the steel mill was cut. (That was back in the early 80's when a lot of people lost their jobs in the mill.) I had no idea how we were going to pay bills or feed the kids. My caseworker at the foodstamp office told me about a food pantry that would help me out until I was approved for food stamps. That was back before "Emergency Food Stamps." The Food Pantry was at a local church. The nice people there offered to help me with my utilities even though I didn't attend their church. Well, that was enough for me! The next Sunday I got my kids ready and we attended that church.

I stopped drinking and refused to go to any more nightclubs to hear my husband's band play. Later that year, Halloween came. Just like every year before, we had a big party at our house and invited all our friends and the whole neighborhood over. We had a keg, lots of booze, and dancing. This year, I didn't drink. I invited a new friend I had just met. She had cancer. I had told her that Jesus could heal her and tried to get her to go to church with me. I was shocked and embarrassed at the behavior of my drunken guests in front of this neighbor and my children. Then one of my neighbors made a pass at me and before I could push him away, my friend said, "I have to leave now!" And she was gone. I just wanted to die!

The next morning as I cleaned up the mess, I cried and vowed this would

47

never happen again. I told God "I am coming back to You completely. This time you can have my <u>ALL</u>! I am going all the way with You!"

I poured all the booze down the drain. I made a new house rule: *"NO MORE BOOZE IN MY HOUSE!"* My husband would have to go somewhere else to do his drinking. I went to church and asked Jesus to come into my heart and change my life. He forgave me of my sins, and my life has never been the same. I am no longer lonely and depressed. I have learned how to be a better mom and wife. I have many wonderful friends who really care about me. I have a peace that passes all understanding.

Two years after I got saved, my husband quit the band and got saved too. WOW! What a change Jesus did in him! He no longer drinks or uses foul language. Even with his job as a supervisor for a large railroad, he has more time for the kids and me than he ever had before he got saved.

You too can experience the life changing power of Jesus Christ. All you have to do is ask God to forgive you of your sins. Ask Jesus to come into your heart and change you into the kind of person He wants you to be. Thank Him for saving you. It's as simple as that! Just say what you want to out loud right now as if He is standing in front of you. He knows you. He hears you. He sees you. He loves you. He wants to help you. He will help you, no matter who you are or what you have done. All you have to do is ask.

— *Miriam*

CHAPTER 16
Is God Mean?

Is God mean? When things go wrong in life, is it God punishing you? I thought so, until...

As a child, I was exposed to God through my family. I was taught to pray and that God existed, nothing more. I thought that God was mean and everything that went wrong was because God was punishing me for something.

When I was 21, I became pregnant. No one really disapproved. At least if they did, they never told me. It seemed okay. Everyone was doing it and had done it. I wasn't married, and that still seemed to be okay. Everyone thought, "Well, at least he's still there."

28 weeks into my pregnancy, something unexpected happened. We were expecting a little girl. The baby and I seemed fine, but on Christmas morning around 3 am, I started feeling sick. I thought it was the cheeseburger I had eaten at 2 am. This stomach ache continued until 8 am. I woke up my boyfriend and my aunt. I wanted to go to the hospital to make sure everything was alright. When we got there, they told me I couldn't go home that day and that I was going to have the baby.

Here I was, three months early, and it was Christmas. Nurses and doctors were everywhere. I was crying. All I could think is that my child was going to die. After nine hours of labor, at 12:43pm, I gave birth to a 2lb., 8oz. crying baby girl. She was whisked away by the neonatal doctor and nurse. I began to call on God. I asked Him to spare her, not knowing all along that this was God's plan. I thought I was being punished for the wrong I did, and that she was going to suffer. The doctor got her

49

stable. They came and told us what was going on. They took her to Methodist Hospital in Gary, and all I could hear was the worst. I checked out of the hospital to go be with her. I called my family and asked them to pray. I prayed and asked the Lord to help her.

She was doing well. The better she got, the less I prayed. I thought, "I prayed and got what I wanted. My part is done." My boyfriend and I went through difficult times after she was born. Things were always difficult, but now we had a baby.

Then, four months after our daughter was born, my boyfriend gave his life to God. He began to change, but I didn't. The Lord placed in his heart that we should get married and live right. So, when our daughter was 18 months old, we got married. I still had not changed much, but God made a promise to my husband that I was unaware of. God told him to pray for my salvation, and I would be saved. Just as God promised, I was saved during my second pregnancy. I began feeling God's love for the first time. I began to understand all that I have been through was for a reason. The reason is to share God's love with others.

If you thought God was mean, if you felt He was punishing you, if you have been through some of the things that I have been through, know this: God loves you and has a good plan for you. He loved you so much that He sent His son Jesus to die on the cross for you.

— *Irene*

CHAPTER 17

Marriage Left Me Bitter And Angry

Marriage left me bitter and angry. I said I would never get married again! Most of my 11 years of marriage were full of verbal abuse, arguing, fighting, and being slapped around. In November 1989, I found out that I was pregnant. I was very happy. I loved children and thought a child would bring me and my husband closer together. However, my husband was not happy at all. In fact, when I told him I was pregnant, he said, "I never wanted any children." The same news that made me so happy only seemed to make him even angrier. All of a sudden he started going out drinking more often. Shortly after that, he started coming home from work, eating dinner, then taking a shower, leaving, and returning home late at night. After a few months of doing this, I finally asked him during dinner one night what was going on. His reply was that he was having an affair.

I was three months pregnant in February 1990. During one of our arguments, he got mad, threw me on the floor, and left bruises on my neck where he choked me. This was the last straw for me. I had enough, and I didn't want my child to have to grow up in an abusive home. I moved out and began to rebuild my life. I said I would never get married again. Marriage left me very bitter and angry at men.

When my son was four years old, I was looking for a good daycare facility for him. I drove past Jubilee Worship Center every day, and one day I noticed a sign, "Day Care Opening Soon." I enrolled my son at the daycare center. I never had any intention of attending a church service at Jubilee Worship Center. I simply wanted a safe place for my son to go to daycare.

I made many good friends at the day care, and one day I was invited by one of the employees to attend church. I went to a couple of services, and they changed my entire life. I asked the Lord into my heart and asked Him to forgive me of my sins. I promised to serve Him and to do my best for the rest of my life.

Over the next several months, God was healing and mending my heart. After eight years of being a single mom, I began having a desire to find a good Christian husband. In 1998, I began to pray that God would send a good Christian man my way. Early in the year, God gave me a vision. Standing off in the distance was my husband and two young children. I knew way down in my spirit that this was the year that I was getting married. I had no one in mind, and I was not dating anyone at this time. I began confessing to people that this was the year I was going to get married. On October 3, 1998, I married the man that God gave to me. I could not have chosen a better man. God is so good.

Friend, if you are going through any of these situations, you need help. You can't fix it on your own. Only God can give you the help you need.

— *Chris*

CHAPTER 18
Work All Day,
Party All Night

Work all day, party all night. Day after day, month after month. Then, I thought, there had to be more to life than this. I don't want to do this any more. I want more out of life. What's missing?

I was 26 years old, living what I thought was a normal life. I would go to work, and then I would go out every night to party with my husband. My husband was an alcoholic. It didn't seem to bother me much until I had decided I didn't want to live that life anymore. I felt there had to be more to life than this.

One day, a lady came into the office where I worked and handed me a New Testament Bible. Since I never had a Bible I was glad to get it.

I was brought up in a Catholic Church, and I faithfully went to church every Sunday. However, I really didn't have a deep understanding of who Jesus was. I started to read the Bible, and it was as if I understood every word. It was like Jesus was speaking to me. I couldn't put it down. I would read it every chance I could.

I noticed that during this time, I started to change. My attitude started changing, and my husband started changing. My husband told me he didn't want to drink anymore. With that news, I wanted to know more and more about God.

In September of 1984, my husband, while he was drunk, went to a small church and asked the pastor to pray for him. On that very night, he was delivered from alcoholism. I knew then how real God was, and I knew Jesus had to be a part of my life.

On Thanksgiving Day in 1984, while watching a Christian station, I prayed the sinner's prayer with the preacher and gave my life to the Lord.

God has not stopped blessing me and changing me since! Glory!!! Do you want more out of life? Do you want Eternal Life?

— *Lupe*

CHAPTER 19
The Smartest
Thing I Ever Did

The smartest thing I ever did. Friend, can I have a few minutes of your time to tell you about the smartest thing I ever did? If you said yes, continue... If you said no, please reconsider...

Have you ever felt totally alone and helpless? Have you ever thought suicide would cure your problems? I HAVE!!! I spent most of my adult life trying to live for me. I was a big time boozer and chased many women in my life. Things just kept getting worse and worse.

I went to several different churches when I was growing up. I did not take church as serious as I should have. I know now that God has always had His hand upon my life. God spared my life in a car accident that should have killed me. Apparently, it was not my time to go. The Lord stayed with me, and finally I heard and listened to His call.

Accepting Jesus as my Lord and Savior was the smartest thing I ever did. Jesus took every burden in my life and gave me a clean slate. The things of the world no longer mattered. Be honest. Wouldn't you like to know that there is someone you can go to 24 hours a day, seven days a week? The Lord is always there. He knows your every problem, and He wants to help if you will allow Him to. God does not try to force Himself on anyone. It is your choice. Please make the right one. He is waiting to hear from you.

Friend, if you have felt alone and helpless, if you have contemplated suicide, if you need help in any way, it's time to do the smartest thing you can. It's time to call out to Jesus.

— Larry

CHAPTER 20
"Please Don't Leave Me Behind!"

"Please don't leave me behind!" These were the words I said as I read a little book that changed my life forever...

When I came to America as a young adult, I thought I was a Christian simply because I knew there was a God. In England during the war, I had to evacuate my home and move to America. In my room was a picture of Jesus that I used to talk to all the time.

After living in America for about a year, a man asked me if I was "born again." Then I had another man come to my door and ask me if I was "saved." I thought these people were really strange. They could have talked all day, and I still would not have understood what they were talking about. I thought to myself, "Born again and saved from what?"

Some years later, my friend asked me to go to church with her. After the service, the preacher gave me a tract on "The Rapture."

After dinner that evening, the children were playing outside, and I picked up the tract. To my surprise, it changed my life! That little book had pictures of planes falling to the ground, trains crashing into each other, people going up to Heaven, and other people who were dead. Looking at the last page, I said to God, "Please don't leave me behind!" In that instant, the Holy Spirit came into my life. I was crying because I was so happy. I wrote a letter to Jesus thanking Him for "saving" my life.

Jesus, the One I used to talk to in the picture, brought me to America just so I could be "Born Again and Saved." Praise God! He had me in His hands all the time.

Friend, I thought I was Christian because I knew there was a God. Knowing there is a God is not enough to get you to heaven.

The devil knows there is a God, and he surely will not be in Heaven. The Bible says the only way to the Father (God) is through the Son (Jesus). The only way that you can someday be with God in Heaven is to receive Jesus Christ, His Son, as your Savior.

Call out to Jesus right now. Confess that He is the Son of God. Confess that He died for you on the cross and arose from the dead. Ask Him to forgive your sins.

— *Dorothy*

CHAPTER 21
Life Started Off Great

Life started off great, but at only 13 years old, I wanted it all to be over...

At the age of 13, I wanted it all to be over. Repressed memories of being molested became unrepressed. I felt worthless and dirty. I hated myself. I became depressed, and life kept spiraling downward. At 14, I started using self-inflicted wounds to release my anger and pain. I became interested in Satanism and Witchcraft. At 15, I was drinking heavily and became suicidal. This continued for another year and a half. On top of this, I poured my problems on top of one another. Sex was not the answer I was looking for either. At 17, I was a mess. It seemed like this life was about to end. Then, at the perfect time, a door opened. God called me to Him. I realized what I was looking for and needed all along was in the scarred face and hands of Jesus! My Savior took me out of nearly five years of depression and hurt. I finally chose to serve Him.

If I could hand it all over to Jesus, you can too. You're never too bad to come to Jesus. He takes us from the world broken, and makes us whole! So what's stopping you?

Come to Jesus today. Call on Jesus, and allow Him to help you.

— *Erin*

58

Penalty For Sin

One day, every man, woman, and child that ever lived will have to pay the price for their sins.

The Bible says:

"For the wages of sin is death."   *Romans 6:23*

Death, meaning eternally (forever) being separated from God. Every person will spend eternity somewhere. Heaven or Hell. (There is no in-between.) You are either with God or the Devil.

The Bible says:

Then the devil who had betrayed them will again be thrown into the Lake of Fire burning with sulphur where the Creature and False Prophet are, and they will be tormented day and night forever and ever.

Revelation 20:10

The Bible also says:

... the corrupt, and murderers, and the immoral, and those conversing with demons, and idol worshipers and all liars — their doom is in the Lake that burns with fire and sulphur: This is the Second Death.

Revelation 21:8

Now, remember your earlier answers to the questions about lying? The Bible says clearly that all liars will be thrown into the Lake of Fire.

At this point, you may be thinking this is hopeless. "I can not obey God's Law." The truth is you can not do it on your own. You need help. God does not want you to face the Fires of Hell and the curse of the Law, and He has provided for you one, and only one chance of escape.

At this point you can go to the next page to read more "Real Life Stories" or turn to page 78 for the next truth.

59

CHAPTER 22
At Only
13 Years Old

At only 13 years old, the desire to fit in and the desire to have friends consumed me and led to many problems...

My problems started when I turned 13. As a child, I had always wanted to fit in, have lots of friends, etc. All kids do. But at age 13, the desire to fit in completely consumed my life. I started smoking because my friends did, and I wanted to look cool. By age 14, alcohol, marijuana, and sex all became a part of my life. My parents had no idea about the alcohol and drugs, but my mom found out about the sex and made me go to the doctor. The doctor told me I had contracted an STD! It was curable, but if it had been left uncured, the disease most likely would have spread and left me infertile. I am so glad my mom found out and made me go to the doctor.

I was grounded for six months after that episode. But I still had to go to school, and my parents had no idea what I was doing at school and during the hours I was supposed to be at school. The downward spiral continued with more drinking, more sex, and more drugs. Boy, did I think I was hot with all these older men following after me. Things progressively got worse.

When I turned 16, my parents bought me a car. I couldn't get my drivers license until 6 months after my 16th birthday, so I was legally only allowed to drive the car with a parent in the front seat. Well, during the summer break from school, my parents were both gone at work all day. So, I snuck the car out on a regular basis. I didn't even have a license. That summer, I ended up overdosing and landed myself in the hospital. All this, even though I was raised in a Christian home by strict parents, who set a good example for me and my younger sister. All this, even though my parents started praying for me before I was even conceived. There wasn't a

60

single day of my life that they didn't pray for me.

When I was released from the hospital, my parents isolated me from all my friends. At first, I was devastated. But it wasn't too long after, I found new friends. I never did drugs again, and I never got into any trouble again. But I still wasn't leading a good life, and I still wasn't walking with the Lord. I was still smoking, having sex, and leading a life of filth.

When I was 19, I met my future husband. He was living the same lifestyle I was. We were definitely equally yoked. Both raised in Christian homes, both living in the ways of the world. Little by little, we cleaned up our acts. Together, we quit smoking. We got married and after a couple years decided to have a baby. We both promised that once we had that baby, we'd get ourselves and our child in church. But we both knew that we were making an empty promise and had no real intentions of going to church.

Then, when I was seven months pregnant, my husband and I had a family crisis. It was a problem that could potentially ruin both of our lives. God grabbed a hold of me and shook me like I've never been shaken before. I knew then that I had to get my life on track. I recommitted my life to the Lord and got myself in church. That huge crisis was suddenly turned to dust. Once I turned my life back to Jesus, He took control of the situation. He patched my wounds, and He healed my scars. My husband got back in church too. It took a couple months, but after our beautiful baby girl was born, he too, realized how important it was for us to have our family in church.

I thank my parents for their continual prayer, and I thank God for every time He helped me. He kept me out of trouble, He kept me alive, He gave me the most wonderful husband, and He gave me the most beautiful child.

Praise You, Jesus!

— Joy

61

CHAPTER 23

I Was Hooked Until....

I started smoking at 14 years old. I started drinking when I was 15 years old. I was arrested for driving under the influence and thrown in jail more times than I could count. I WAS HOOKED UNTIL....

I started smoking when I was 14 and drinking when I was 15. Whenever I could drink beer, I would. Between 18 and 30 years old, I had been arrested for D.U.I. so many times I couldn't count. I was put in jails from Portage to Munster.

In 1984, I was 34 years old, and my wife became a Born Again Christian. I was so tired of drinking and being a bum. I don't know how many times I quit drinking. It was usually during a hangover. I called up the minister that had married my wife and I. I asked him if he would talk to me about my drinking. This was on a Thursday night, and I was drunk. He met me at the church around midnight and he talked and prayed with me. I asked God to deliver me from drinking. And He did! I haven't had a drink since that night.

In 1986, My wife's associate pastor came over one night to visit with us. He asked me if I wanted to accept God into my life, and I said yes. I became a Christian that very night.

I also wanted to quit smoking, but that proved to be a bigger challenge. I had quit numerous times, and I had used every device advertised on T.V. to help me. I never asked God to help me. That's where I made my mistake!

We started attending church in 1997. I was really having a problem with smoking. I felt the Holy Spirit talking to me about my smoking. I finally asked God to deliver me from cigarettes. For four and a half years I have been smoke free. Praise the Lord.

My big mistake in life was not asking for Gods help. Do not make that mistake. Call out for God to help you right now. He will help you just as He helped me.

— *Steve*

CHAPTER 24
16 Years Old
And Pregnant

16 years old and pregnant. I lived in a dysfunctional home full of drugs and drinking, which led to:

Cigarettes at age 12
Marijuana at age 13
Drinking at age 14
Sex at age 15
Pregnancy at age 16

I thought I could never change my lifestyle until...

I was 16, pregnant, living in a home full of drugs, doing drugs, drinking, and thought I could never change my life. I was looking for love in all the wrong places. I started having sex at 15 and ending up getting pregnant. Even though I knew I was pregnant, I hid it from everyone around me and even tried to lie to myself.

I finally began to accept my pregnancy and set up a doctor's appointment, but the morning before my visit, I woke up with blood at my feet. I went to the doctor to find out what was happening. He said that I was 13 weeks pregnant and having a miscarriage. He said I needed to go to the hospital, but I refused to go because I didn't want my parents to know. Finally, after a week of miscarrying, I told my mom and my dad. My dad arranged for me to go to the hospital, and after all the tests they said everything was fine.

Looking back now, I realize why I was having sex at such a young age. My home, the place where I looked to find all my security, was so dysfunctional. Ever since my parents divorced when I was in kindergarten, I have lived with my mom and her crack-cocaine habit. Throughout all of my young childhood, my mom hid her habit from me. Then, in time, it took over her body and eventually started running her life and making her careless. I felt that I could not tell my mom that she was doing wrong because I had already been smoking cigarettes since I was 12, marijuana since 13, drinking since 14, and then got pregnant at 16.

Finally, my mom was so consumed with drugs that she started to bring it home. Soon, there were drug dealers hanging out there all the time. We had no money, no food, and our bills were left unpaid. My mom found herself selling crack to support her habit. She would make close to $2000 some days, but we didn't have the money to pay the rent or have food in the house. Soon, I too started selling drugs to pay the rent and to take care of my mom, myself, and our home, our "crack-house" home. This went on for a good eight or nine months. I was scared. I knew I was being watched by the cops 24-7. Once, I walked in the door, and about three minutes later some guys came running into my house with shotguns, demanding drugs and money. Then on October 3, 2002, after living under heavy surveillance for a long time, my house was raided. I was slammed on the ground like I was a 200 lb. man. There were about 20 indictments on people from my town. This included my mom, my boyfriend who was living with me, my sister's boyfriend, and many other people I was close to. Through all of this, now when I look back, I realize that God gave me many chances that I was not worthy of. When I lost the baby, I looked at it as a bad thing. Now I realize that God was giving me a second chance to live my life, just like He gave me a second chance after the drugs. I didn't get away with selling drugs because I was good or just didn't get caught. I'm not in jail right now because God had a better plan for my life. I gave my life to the Lord, and day by day, just like a newborn child, I'm learning. I'm learning to crawl and before you know it, I'll be taking my first steps and afterwards running. Isn't the Lord great!

Friend, if you were born into a dysfunctional home and surrounded by drugs and alcohol like I was, you can let it control your life or you can break that dysfunctional cycle today by crying out for help like I did. Call on Jesus right now. Ask Him to forgive your sins. Ask Him to give you a new life. Ask Him to come into your life and live in your heart.

— *Kassie*

65

CHAPTER 25

Divorce Devastated
My Life

Divorce devastated my life. I was unhappy, confused, unloved, abandoned, let down, and hurt as I wandered through the maze of life. Until....

My parents were very young when they got married. My mom was only 16. Both of my parents had grown up in Christian homes. Growing up, my parents taught me about God. However, knowing about God and being raised in a Christian home did not exclude us from the devastation of divorce.

I loved my parents, but I felt as if they had let me down. When I was only four years old, my parents divorced. Life for me would never be the same again. Shortly after the finalization of their divorce, my mother began going out a lot. She also did a lot of entertaining in our home. She had no idea that the decisions she was making would affect my life so strongly. I saw and was surrounded by things that would rob any child of his innocence. It did not stop there. It was not long before I too allowed the devastation of my parents' divorce to consume my every move. I suffered physical and sexual abuse from close friends and family. Then, I turned to drugs and alcohol and allowed them to take over my life.

I became very confused and lonely. I wanted desperately to feel loved and wanted. In this search, sex became a normal part of my life. My virginity was lost at the tender age of 16. Something was missing in my life and so much had gone wrong. My boyfriend's cousin invited me to church one Sunday. I went, and on that day I gave my heart to God. However, I did not really understand what God had done for me that day. It wasn't long before I again turned to sex, searching for fulfillment in my life, desperately desiring to feel wanted and needed.

I knew there was something missing in my life, and there was an urgency to find what I had been missing for so long. It took me a long time to realize that I was searching in all the wrong places.

In my search and desperation, I tried going out to crazy parties. I once again turned to drugs. I had been with men and learned that they only let me down. I began experimenting with women only to discover that perverse relationships led to the same feelings of hurt and rejection that my relationships with men had.

My life was getting worse and worse, crazier and crazier. My heart had been broken over and over again. I felt so alone. The things I had learned about God at a young age, and the love He had for me often came to my mind. However, guilt would come over me, and then I would think to myself, "How could God love me, the girl who was guilty of every sin in the book, and who was now pregnant, and not married?"

My pregnancy only led to more confusion and frustration. I argued with my boyfriend all through the pregnancy. I cried, and I was hurting. When the baby came and I held him in my arms for the first time, I could only cry tears of shame and not of joy for what I had done to this baby's life. I was unmarried and miserable and had brought another life into the misery I was living.

After my little boy was born, I decided that I wanted a new start for my son and for myself. I started going to church again. God took me back and loved me more than I had ever been loved by any man. I understood John 3:16 "For God so loved the world that He gave His only son that whosoever believes in Him should not perish but have everlasting life."

Understanding this verse was the first step for me in actually comprehending God and accepting His love for me.

My boyfriend and I argued more because I was trying so hard to please God. I struggled for five or six months. In a desperate attempt to hold onto the man who was now my husband, I began drifting away from the Lord. Instead of leaning on God, I leaned on my husband, the father of my now two precious little boys.

During my second pregnancy I thought a lot about God and what He had previously done for me. I wanted to have a relationship with God. I missed the way He made me feel. I began to pray and ask God to send me to a church where I could be with Him, a church where I could grow and learn about Him and experience His Spirit.

What a miracle it was that when I found a childcare center for my boys, I also found a church that I could attend. On Easter Sunday, I went to that church. They played beautiful songs that made it so easy to open up to God. There was a play about Jesus that moved me to tears. At the end of the service, the pastor asked if anyone would like to ask Jesus to come into their heart and let Him be their Lord and Savior. I felt a big tug in my heart and knew right away that God was talking to me. I ran to the front of the church and asked God for His mercy and forgiveness. God once again filled the void in my life. He gave me His love again. I have given up on God and gone away so many times in my life, but He was always there.

It took me a long time to realize that God loved me all along, and I want to share that same message with you. God loves us no matter what we have done, who we have been with, or what has been done to us. He was waiting for me all that time, and He is waiting for you, too. God is faithful, even when we are unfaithful. He loves you just like He loves me. His Love is forever, and His love will never stop. His Love never hurts you or causes you to feel shame. His love never leaves you searching and empty because in Him, you will find everything.

Maybe at some point in your life, you felt the way I did: unhappy, confused, unloved, abandoned, let down, hurt, and wandering through a maze that seems to have no end.

I was looking and searching for what I thought was something material, only to find that all along, I was looking for Jesus. He has all the details of my life worked out, and He is working everything out for my good. He wants to do the same for you!

— *Diana*

CHAPTER 26

I Was Consumed With Guilt

I was consumed with guilt. When I would drive by familiar places or see familiar things, I would remember my past, and guilt would make me sick to my stomach. When I could take it no more, I...

When I asked God to help me and to come into my life I had a lot of excess baggage I brought with me. I had 22 years of sin that had been piling up inside me. I couldn't carry that burden any longer. It was too much. I knew that I really needed help. I had sunk to the lowest point I had ever been in my life. I had been involved in drugs and alcohol for most of those 22 years. For the last 10 years I had lived over 1,000 miles away from home, and away from all my family and friends. When I woke up (or you might say when I grew up), I was surrounded by strangers. All of them were as bad as me, if not worse. Help was not in sight, or so I thought.

I called home and spoke to my mother. She reminded me that there was help. She reminded me that my help had never left me, even though I had left it. I called upon God to help me out of the mess I had made of my life. I had forgotten how simple and easy it was to ask for God's help. He heard my cry, and in time, things worked out. I returned home to God and to my family.

It was then that I faced the biggest challenge of my life! This was bigger than the temptation of drugs and alcohol, which was constantly being thrown in my face. God delivered me from that, and the Devil could no longer use it on me, so he went to work on other ways to bring me down. The biggest obstacle I faced was GUILT. That was the method of choice that the Devil used on me. When I returned home and back in church, things weren't easy.

I went through many trials. I have a favorite saying, "What doesn't kill you will make you stronger."

I was getting stronger in the Lord, but the Devil worked overtime placing guilt on me to get me back in his control. I would drive by familiar places where I had done a lot of partying. I would have this guilt come over me that would make me sick to my stomach. Satan would bring to memory all the sinful things I had done, said, and thought. This overwhelming guilt was eating away at me. I thought I would have to leave the area to get peace.

After I thought I couldn't take it any more, I asked God to help me. I told God that if this is where He wanted me to be, He would have to help me. God took away the guilt. I look back now and think how Satan kept me down by making me think that I had sinned too much and that I was not worthy to come back into God's presence again. I always felt I had to clean up first before I came to Him. I felt I had too much baggage and too much guilt to get rid of.

God does not expect us to get rid of anything or to clean ourselves up before we come to Him. That is His job, and I realize now that He loves me that much. He gives us the help. He does the cleaning up, and He gets rid of the baggage and guilt for us. We only have to ask Him. The Devil would like to keep you down too. He makes us think that it's too much or that it's too hard. He makes us think we're too bad and we're not worthy. DON'T LET HIM FOOL YOU!!! It's lonely down there, and the Devil wants company. If you have guilt that overwhelms you and holds you down, I know someone who can take it away, renew your spirit, and make you whole again.

— *Jenny*

71

CHAPTER 27

My Heart
Was Broken

My heart was broken. I cried for months. A little girl told me something that I never forgot...

I was 21 years of age and about to make the biggest decision of my life. I was involved in a 9-year relationship with a woman who did not quite believe as much as I did. In fact, I think she believed in God just enough to keep me believing that God was in control. I grew up in a dysfunctional, unstable home with three older siblings, all who wanted to be on their own. This 9-year relationship gave me the stability I longed for as a child.

With two sisters and one brother all older than me, I always seemed to catch the "after-shock" of everything that took place in our lives. The large age gap between my brothers and sisters caused me to fair for myself and figure things out on my own. This forced sense of self-dependence later led to my adventurous personality and a desire for love and acceptance, causing me to leave early in the morning and not return until the late evening, searching for fulfillment.

I have always known that my parents loved me the best way they knew how, but there was still an emptiness that I was searching to fill. I had been raised in church and had been taught about God my entire life, but at this point, everything I had learned was just more words. I did not take God's Word for what it was worth. I simply looked at them as words in a leather-bound book.

While in this search for fulfillment, I found nothing at church, so I decided to look elsewhere. I turned to relationships. In the 7th and 8th grade, I found myself in a very serious relationship with a young lady who smothered me with affection. The attention and affection she gave me began to fill the emptiness. I was only in Junior High, and I thought I was complete. But like most things in life, all good things must come to an end. Our relationship was in and out, up and down, but I did not want to let her go. Our relationship was a comfort to me. It had become my stability.

Letting her go was very difficult for me. It broke my heart and left me crying for months. When we broke up, that little girl told me something that I have never forgotten. She told me, "If you love something, let it go. If it doesn't come back to you, it was never meant to be. If it does come back, then it is yours forever." I had lost my stability in life and began hurting all over again. The only way I knew to make it stop was to find another girl and get in another relationship to heal my brokenness.

At the end of my freshman year, I started dating another girl. It began just as something to fill the void, but soon became very comfortable. She met all my needs; physically and emotionally. We dated through high school and after graduation. Since we had been together for so long, I thought I ought to make it official and marry her. It had been nine years, and I didn't think either of us was going anywhere anytime soon.

I thought my life was finally going to be complete. I knew I needed to get a house, which I did. Then I got everything else in order that needed to be done before we could get married. We set the date, booked the hall, ordered invitations, ordered dresses, and did just about everything else we needed. We were set, and we were happy. As time drew closer to the wedding, the emptiness began to come back. Along with the emptiness came sadness, depression, and unfulfillment. I didn't understand what was happening.

I was attending church faithfully, but I was just going through the motions and never really giving it my all. Then one day, the Spirit of the Lord began to move, and all I could do was cry. I cried through the entire service, as if I had been suppressing my feelings all my life. It felt good to release all the bottled emotions, but I knew from this point on, my life would never be the same. I began to examine my life, my fiancée's life, and our relationship. Doubt began to set in, and fear gripped my heart. I felt that if God called me into the ministry, she would not be strong enough to support me. I was nervous, confused, and without answers. My family gave their opinions, but I knew God had a reason for what he was doing, and that He was capable of doing anything.

I spoke with my pastor several times. He was very supportive with any decision that I could make, but made it very clear that it was my decision to make no matter what anyone else said. I was still in the dark, without any answers. I wanted someone to tell me what I should do. I wanted a plain and simple yes or no. I knew God was on my side and would work my decision out for my good, so three weeks before the wedding, we called everything off.

I was alone again and hurting. My stability was gone, and those who supported my decision I felt had abandoned me. I couldn't understand why God was allowing this to hurt so bad. I made the decision He wanted me to, so why didn't He take the pain and hurt away?

My loneliness and pain forced me to take matters into my own hands. I began seeing my former fiancée on and off again. I got mad at God because He was capable of doing anything, but He wouldn't fix my relationship. I was mad at church people because they failed to take the time to build up and disciple the woman I wanted to be my future wife.

I became very sick and depressed. Thoughts of suicide crossed my mind. I decided that if serving God caused so much pain, I wanted nothing to do with Him or the people who served Him. The only reason I continued to go to church during this four-year depression was to avoid going to Hell.

I became afraid of commitment and relationships. I promised myself I would never allow myself to get hurt like that again. I began to treat women like they treated me. I played with their emotions, promising them the world. I would shower them with gifts, take them all back, then move on to the next one. I didn't care if they were single or married. I talked to any woman I could get my hands on. But deep inside me, there was a small voice that convicted me of my wrongs.

I reached a point in my life where I was going to get back with my ex-fiancée, and there was nothing that God or anyone else could do to stop me. I was going to marry that girl once and for all. Unfortunately, she didn't feel the same way. She was tired of all my broken promises. I was angry and became violent about the things of God because I wanted her back so bad. I tried everything. I even used my 8th-grade girl-friend to maker her jealous, because I knew how my ex-fiancée felt about her.

People always said that I would one day marry my 8th-grade girlfriend. But I always told them that she was one marriage and two kids too late for me. As she and I began hanging out together, we became really good friends. We went to church together because that is where we had met again. As a kid, I always said I would marry her, but after the lifestyle she lived and what her life had become, I never thought it would happen.

I started getting back in church and finding my love for the Lord one more time. It took nothing short of a miracle to get me back to the things of God because I had allowed my hurt and pain to control me for so long. It took me a long time to realize that through it all, God was there. He said He would never leave me nor forsake me. It was my choices that caused the pain in my life. I know now that my life would have been much easier if I would have left matters in His hands, in-stead of my own.

God has put a love back in my life for "that little girl," to whom I am now married. I have never had a closer relationship in my life than I do now. I have never been in love with God like I am now. It was a long road traveled, but I have arrived and plan on staying forever. I am in my home church of twenty years and don't plan on moving until the Lord is ready to move me.

I now know that which hurts you can only make you stronger. I have learned to trust in God with all my heart and lean not on my own understanding, in all my ways I acknowledge Him and He makes my path straight. I am the man

75

I am today because God never gave up on me. Even when I threw in the towel and gave up, God was still there with open arms. He has given us the roadmap of life.

You can choose the easy way or the hard way. Either way, He's going to get you where He needs you!

Friend, we all need help. We were not created to go it alone. Whatever your need is, my Friend is here to help you.

— *Rich*

CHAPTER 28

I Was
Depressed...

I was depressed... I was angry... I drank to forget... Things kept getting worse... Until...

I had the same job for 20 years. The bank I worked for was being sold again. Having a house, a wife, and two children, I felt I was a failure. I was depressed and very angry. I drank to forget, but the drinking just made me angrier and even more depressed. The problems were still there day after day, and the drinking did not make me forget. I took out my anger and frustration on my family. On February 3, 1998, my wife finally had enough. She asked me to leave our home. Shortly thereafter, she filed for a divorce. I had two options at this point. I could move in with one of my drinking buddies, or I could move in with my sister. My sister had one stipulation for me living with her. If I lived with her, I had to go to church with her. I chose to live with my sister. This was when my life began to change. On February 8, 1998, I accepted the Lord Jesus Christ as my savior. It was as if the monkey (Satan) was finally off my back.

In July 1998, the Lord put a beautiful, wonderful, and loving woman at my side. We were married October 3, 1998.

Jesus has a plan for your life. Won't you accept Him into your life?

— Ed

God's Love

God loved His creation (you) so much that He sent His Son to earth to pay the full price for all sin.

Jesus did not come to the earth to do away with God's law. He came to fulfill it.

Jesus came as a man in the flesh and did not sin. Not one time. He obeyed the commandments, God's Law. Fully. He did for you what you could never do.

Jesus was beaten, tortured, and hung on a cross. While on that cross, the sins of the world (your sins) were placed on His shoulders.

Jesus died for and with your sins, but death could not hold Him; the grave could not contain Him. He arose from that grave paying the full price for every person's sin. (That includes you.)

It is only through God's Love, God's Mercy, and God's Grace that we can escape the curse of the law.

From here, you can go to the next page for more "Real Life Stories," or skip to page 95 for more truth.

CHAPTER 29
Are You Insecure?

Are you insecure? Can marriage give you security? Can having children give you security? Is there a solution for insecurity? Yes! There is! And I have found where I belong...

I know what insecurity is, for I have been insecure for most of my life. It was this feeling of insecurity that led me to my first marriage. I thought that marriage would be the key that would open the door to the security and happiness that I was longing for. But it did not take long for me to come to the realization that, though I loved my husband, nothing had changed. He was not able to free me from the grip of this tormenting insecurity. In time, we had a beautiful baby girl, and she was the joy of our lives. I found a measure of fulfillment in raising her, but the insecurity, even though it was subdued for a time, was still a very real presence in my life. When my husband passed away after a fifteen-year battle with kidney failure, I was devastated and my insecurities only became intensified. Our only daughter, in the meantime, had been diagnosed as a "special needs" child. But she prospered and at age eighteen was able to move into supervised living quarters where she can enjoy some independence. It was not too long after this that I met a wonderful man, and we had sixteen memorable years together. During this time, it seemed that my insecurities had gone into remission. And they had, until he too was taken from me. Now utter hopelessness compounded my insecurities. But that's not the end of the story. My next door neighbor showed up at my door one day and asked me to go to church with her. I had not been a church-goer, and the few times I had gone, I felt it was irrelevant to my life. So it came as a complete surprise to me when I heard myself saying, "yes." On the second Sunday that I went with her, the pastor prayed for me, and I was saved!

Afterward, I was fearful and wondered what I had gotten myself into. My neighbor and two other ladies from church took me under their wing. Between the three of them, they were able to calm my fears and answer all of the many questions that were racing through my mind. They have been there for me ever since, no matter what my need has been.

As I look back over my life and the ins and outs of my insecurities, I can see that God was there all the time, weaving the pattern that would bring me to Him. Even though insecurities still try to invade my life, my searching days are over... as the song says, "I found where I belong."

If you are overwhelmed with insecurities as I was, only God can deliver you. He is the answer to all your problems. Don't wait to be asked; just go to a church. God is waiting for you. He will become the most relevant person in your life. Don't just go for a time or two; keep going until you know you are set free. By that time, you won't want to stop going!

Jesus is our Savior! Our only Savior! He can be your Savior, too. John 3:16 says, "For God so loved the world, that He gave His only begotten Son, that whosoever believes in Him shall not perish, but have everlasting life." Just believe in Him. Accept Him as your Lord and Savior, and He can give you confidence and assurance for your doubts and insecurities.

— *Pat*

CHAPTER 30
I Tried To
Commit Suicide

I tried to commit suicide. When it seemed like I would never find someone that really loved me, I found a true friend who will never leave me.

I was raised in a home filled with problems. My mother abused and mistreated me, which led me to feel unloved, lonely, and rejected by the most important person in my life. Growing up, my parents were very strict, and they didn't let us associate with other people.

I got married at the age of 16 because I was searching for love and wanted to leave home. Because I was young at the time, I didn't understand a lot of things, so it took me awhile to realize I was looking for love in all the wrong places.

After eight years of marriage and three children, I left my alcoholic, abusive husband. After I left, I continued searching for love in various relationships. I was later introduced to the world of drugs and alcohol. I soon discovered that although I didn't feel any pain and nothing seemed to bother me while I was on drugs, I still felt so empty on the inside. I became so deep into sin that I tried to take my own life on three different occasions.

On one of those attempts, I had everything ready to end my life when, all of a sudden, my telephone rang. It was one of my sisters in Puerto Rico. Once she realized what I was trying to do, she begged me not to. Then suddenly, we were disconnected. She immediately called me back and began to pray and rebuke the devil. At that moment, peace flooded my life. The feelings of desperation and thoughts of suicide left my mind, and I began to cry. It was then that I understood that God had a plan for my life, and why after three attempts, I had not succeeded in taking my life.

There was a time in my life when I would go to bars to meet men who would cause me pain and misery. But now, after the new-found peace, I was at a loss. I didn't know what to do or where to go. I didn't know that all this time my family was praying for me.

It wasn't long before God sent my sister Elsa to invite me to attend church with her. When I heard the message, it seemed as if the pastor was speaking to me. I started to cry and couldn't contain myself. When he made the altar call, I couldn't move. Something was holding me to my seat. There was war in my mind. I didn't go to the altar at that time, but I kept visiting the church. It seemed like every time I would go to church, I would cry a lot. Yet, I refused to adhere to God's call.

I continued participating in worldly things and felt convicted for what I was doing, but I headed for the path of destruction once more. During this time, I made my children suffer a lot. I did things I never thought I would do, but I still could not find the "love" that I was looking for.

Since I only attended school up to the eighth grade, I had to go to work in a nursing home. I became very involved with my work helping the elderly, and I would forget about my problems. It wasn't long before I met my second husband, who I thought "loved" me. But this marriage failed too.

After my second marriage failed, I went back to church with my sister. This time, the Lord spoke to my sister, and she took me to the altar. As they prayed for me, I felt this heavy load I had been carrying lift off me. On that day, I found Jesus who loved me and accepted me for who I was. He opened His arms and made me feel that I was worth something. He has changed my life. Now I have a friend who never turns His back on me or rejects me. Even when I miss it because I am not perfect, He is there with His open arms. My children began attending church with me. The Lord is working in their lives. Even though they don't all serve the Lord, I know and trust God is going to change them. Now, the Lord is my strength and my fortress. He has blessed me abundantly. I can't imagine my life without

Christ. If you have searched and searched for love and found hurts and heartaches like I did, you need to look in the right place. Jesus is the answer, and He has been waiting for you to call on Him.

— *Ana*

CHAPTER 31
Daddies Don't Do
Things Like That!

Daddies don't do things like that! My relationships were always sexually, verbally, and physically abusive. I started getting into witchcraft, tarot cards, and ouija boards. Then I saw the way that things are supposed to be...

When I was little, I had a really close relationship with God. I had received the baptism of the Holy Spirit at three years old. You know how some people have imaginary friends? Well, Jesus was mine. I saw him all the time. When I was ten, I was baptized and gave devotionals during service almost every Sunday.

When I hit puberty, my step-dad molested me. I questioned God, "How could you let him do this to me?" Daddies don't do things like that." My mother did not believe me. She thought it was all in my head. She used my relationship with God to rationalize what my step-dad had done. She said that the could not believe that I was growing up. He had to see for himself. She told me God wanted me to forgive him and to forget about what had happened. From that night on I slept with my door locked. I stopped going to church. I started listening to the Sex Pistols. Anarchy was my middle name. Two years later, he did it again. He broke the lock on my door. He violated me. I couldn't and didn't accept this. When I got to school, I called my family in Indiana and they told my mom. My mother moved us 30 miles away from him. Yet she still had a relationship with him. On my 13th birthday, my mother made me kiss him on the cheek because he gave me money as a present. After we ate the cake, my sister went to work. I was left home alone on my birthday while my mom was with my step-dad at his home. I was hurt that my mother would leave me on my birthday to spend time with the man who had hurt me. That was the first time I tried to take my life. I did not know I didn't take enough Tylenol to succeed. God spared my life.

My mother had just found out that my step-dad had been with another woman a year after he had molested me. She then wanted to press charges. She only wanted to press charges then because he said he wanted to have both of us and that if he couldn't have us both, then he didn't want her. I can now forgive my mom for all the things that have happened. But, because of these horrible things, I have lived my life on the edge. The edge caught up with me. Every relationship that I have had has been sexually, verbally, and physically abusive. I started getting into witch-craft, tarot cards, and ouija boards. I always knew that God was still with me. I just thought that I wasn't good enough to serve Him. I had three children, and my marriage failed. I tried to kill myself twice because I was so deeply depressed.

After my marriage failed, I became promiscuous and drank heavily. I experimented with drugs, but justified my actions. I decided that my actions were okay because I never brought it around my children. After all, my husband introduced me to this lifestyle. I only did it when my kids were at their dad's. I met my boyfriend at a bar. We had dated for a year and a half. I thought that he was very supportive of me. Then, I saw the way that things were supposed to be. My sister in law invited me to church, and God began to plant a seed in my heart. I saw her get married to the love of her life. The love they had for God was stronger than any love that they could have had for each other. When I saw them get married, I knew that was what I wanted. I got saved on Palm Sunday and started going to church. I kicked my boyfriend out because that is what I felt God wanted me to do. That was exactly right. My boyfriend came back, and I let him in. I let him sleep on the couch, and before long he was back in my bed. The closer I got to my boyfriend, the further I got from God. When you don't do things the way God wants you to, they never work. I broke up with my boyfriend on my birthday. We got into a physical fight. He has not been in my bed since. I didn't do it for God. I did it for me. I still drank and partied. When I heard Christian music, I changed the station. Before long, my life came crashing down. I was at a bar and I was very drunk. Someone offered me some ecstasy. Instead of taking it, I put it in my pocket. I tried to give it away and found out the hard way that he was a police officer. I spent four nights in jail. I spent that time on my knees. I have never been on my knees

85

so much in my life. I let God down, my family down, and my children down. How could I do something like that?

How could I make it better? All I could do is pray. My ex-husband tried to take my children away from me. He let me see them for three hours on a Sunday. I went straight to church with them. I prayed with the pastor for my children and for my salvation. He told me it would not be easy, and that I have to walk the walk and mean it. I had to give my children back to my ex-husband and assure my children that everything was going to be okay. The next day I had court, and the judge was going to let my ex-husband keep my children, until I testified. I knew that my children were coming home with me because I prayed and did not doubt Him. The judge had me take a drug test right then and there. I knew I would pass. When the judge got the results back that I had passed, he said "Give her back her children." I got on my knees in that courtroom and praised Jesus. The judge just looked at me in amazement. Then after thanking Jesus, I thanked the judge. God has blessed me so abundantly. I now live a Christian lifestyle, and it is the best thing that has ever happened to me. God has delivered me from alcohol, drugs, depression, and cigarettes. He has changed my life and made me new again. I have a new beginning. I have a new life. I have a peace in my heart. I know that no matter what happens to me, God will always love me. That is the best feeling in the world. God desires to change your life too. Take the time today and choose Jesus. He is the only way to really be free.

If you want Jesus to save you from all your pain and all your heartache, let Him into your heart right now.

— *Charlotte*

CHAPTER 32
Sex, Drugs, And Rock & Roll

Sex, Drugs, and Rock & Roll. I was depressed and confused when sober, so I tried to stay high all the time. My mother noticed a change in me. She thought I was high on drugs, but I wasn't. I was high on...

I was saved at around 9 or 10 years of age. At 13 years old, we moved to a new town, and I stopped going to church. Then things got worse. I started smoking, doing drugs, and having sex at 14. For the next five years sex, drugs, and rock & roll was my motto.

I was depressed and confused when sober, so I tried to stay high. I couldn't deal with reality. My home was not a peaceful place. Being the oldest of five children, much responsibility was placed on my shoulders. There was almost no relationship with my father, and I was at war with my mother much of the time.

As a teen, I started rebelling against any responsibility toward the family. I didn't even want to get married or have children because of all the problems that were in our family and extended family.

At 17 years old, I met a guy I fell head over heels for. His parents were spirit-filled Christians who really lived the Christian life. Their home was so peaceful, and they really seemed to like me. After I had been dating their son for awhile, they invited me to church. We would go sometimes out of respect and love for them. I don't remember much about it other than the love all those people showed to me. We dated for two years before things got bad. He proposed to me and then changed his mind because his parents weren't in agreement. I was so hurt that I began being unfaithful behind his back. Eventually, he became suspicious and found out.

I was losing the one person I had given my whole heart to, and there was nothing I could do to change it or take it back. I FELT LIKE ALL THAT WAS LEFT TO DO WAS LAY DOWN AND DIE!!!

In the meantime, his parents told him to give me a Good News Bible then read it and pray for God to forgive me for all my sins. I began reading the Bible in the book of Matthew for the very first time in my life. It was amazing because at that time in my life, I HATED to read, but I couldn't seem to put it down.

My family took me on a vacation for a week, far away from all the problems back home. This helped a lot, and there were no distractions. I spent three days repenting. Something inside of me was changing. My younger sisters thought I was becoming nicer.

I thought there might be hope of reconciliation with my boyfriend if I did everything he was telling me to do. Of course, that was not the case. Eventually it was clear that the relationship could not be worked out. Before everything was completely over, he kept wanting something from God called the Baptism in the Holy Spirit. I had no idea what that was, but I quickly decided that if he thought it was so great, I wanted it too!

One night in my own home, I simply asked God for the baptism of the Holy Spirit, and He gave it to me. I still didn't know exactly what had happened to me or what it meant, but it sure felt good. I had an explosion of love bursting forth from my heart. My mother even noticed it and thought I was high on drugs again, but I wasn't ... I WAS HIGH ON JESUS! I experienced many miracles during this time. I no longer had a desire for cigarettes or any kind of drug.

Since then, there has been many struggles and trials in my life, but God gave me the power to walk through them with Him. My parents are Christians now, and they are serving the Lord. Through much prayer, many of my family members are Christians now too. If you need peace in your life like I did, call out for help today. Call on the Peace Maker.

— *Marla*

CHAPTER 33

"Free Gift"

Many years ago, my wife and I settled down to raise a family. My wife met some great people at the church where we were married, and I believe this was the start of my receiving the "Free Gift" that I am talking about.

Over the years our family grew. We had four wonderful children, a fantastic marriage, financial success, and many good friends. Sounds good, doesn't it? Even though it was good, I had many questions.

Why am I here? What is life about? Is it possible to live — just to die? What good is financial success when we must die? Why do it? Why even be here? Why do I feel so confused? What is the answer? Why, when I have so much, do I have a feeling of emptiness?

For 19 years, I strongly believed that my family was the only thing that mattered and I set out to provide my family with everything the world had to offer. Almost everything I did was geared to provide for my family and generations of family to come. Also, during this period of time, I searched high and low, trying many things, to fill the emptiness or void I felt: playing softball with the guys and drinking after the games, playing racquetball and drinking after the games, buying campers, snowmobiles, new cars, houses, etc. I tried working extra hours to make more money, buying more worldly possessions, starting a business, investing in and buying real estate, etc, etc, etc. All of these things gave me a very short-lived pleasure or happiness that would not last! It would leave as quick as it came.

Fortunately for my family, while I was providing for their worldly life, my wife, Carla, was building the foundation for our eternal life. I have always believed there was a God and I would occasionally pray when things were so far out of my control that I could not fix them. A couple things come to mind — like when my daughter was only weeks old and we had to put her in the hospital and I feared for her life; also, when my son lay in the hospital with a staph infection; and finally, when my wife was very sick and had an infection in her blood system — the doctor told me that my wife only had a 50/50 chance of survival. The most recent time was when a friend called for our support when his father was very ill. Carla went to help our friend while I stayed home with the kids.

As I laid there in bed that morning, I told GOD that I felt my friend's father was still needed in this world and that there was much good he could do by teaching God's word to people like me that still needed help. I asked GOD to please save my friend's father and to give him the opportunity to help others like myself. In return, I promised to try to follow his path, starting with attending church that coming Sunday.

The following Sunday, I attended church with my wife and it was a very peaceful feeling. The people at church all seemed so happy and full of life that it made me want to return the next Sunday. As the service was ending on my second visit, I felt very relaxed and was in no hurry to leave. After searching for the answers to my earlier questions, I came to the conclusion that we could not possibly live just to die. There was no other answer or reasoning to my problems and questions other than believing in God and having enough faith to accept His Son Jesus Christ in my life, so I did!

The love I saw in all the people "hit me" and it was like nothing else I have ever felt in my life. At that time I was not sure if it was Jesus filling the empty place in my heart or just all the love of the people reaching out to me, but whatever it was, I hoped it would never stop. And if I could have one prayer answered, it would be that all God's people have the opportunity to share the same experiences that I have come to enjoy, need, and want.

Looking back, I know that the Lord was with me every step of the way, and the path He was leading me down was to teach me about the values of the world and temporary happiness versus complete and total joy and the values of the Lord. The Lord blessed me and my family by enabling us to make the right decisions in regard to my investments. I have always based my decisions on what I called my "gut feeling," but now I know it was my inner spirit leading me to worldly prosperity so that I would some day be able to testify that the things of the world are temporary and that worldly happiness will slip away very quickly.

Even though I was blessed with prosperity before being blessed as a Christian, being a Christian means more to me than anything the world has to offer. Recently my wife and I were approached by a lady we did not know and she asked us to pray for her heart problem. She said she could see that we were Christians. Being recognized as a Christian was one of the best moments of my life.

If you have any of the questions or problems I had, don't try to weather the storm on your own, come in out of the rain and let the Son of God, Jesus, meet your every need. Let Him lead you and guide you, through the Holy Spirit, from now to eternity. Since the writing of this testimony, the empty place in my heart has been permanently filled with the Love of my Savior, Jesus Christ, the Holy Spirit, and God our Father.

In 1990 I had to quit my job of almost 20 years due to a rare blood disease. The doctors did not know what caused it and said they could do nothing for me. In January of 1994 the Lord told me He was going to heal me of that rare blood disease. In March of 1994, I took the same blood test that had led to the diagnosis that I had the rare disease. This time the results were negative! My blood had been cleansed by the Blood of My Savior. By His stripes I was healed. Praise God! God can meet your every need, and will if you do your part. I urge you to read God's word daily, pray daily, praise the Lord's name daily, and go to church every time the door is open.

"If ye abide in me, and my words abide in you, ye shall ask what you will, and it shall be done unto you." John 15:7

Receive the "FREE GIFT" – God Bless You, Jim

91

CHAPTER 34
My Life Was Like
Murphy's Law!

My life was like Murphy's Law! Anything that could go wrong would go wrong. Until I found true peace and joy through... Jesus. This is my story:

I am 46 years old and single. I'm sitting here wondering where to begin. My mother and father divorced when I was real young. To this day, I really don't know why. Those are things that we never asked or talked about. What I do remember, is that my life was never a good one. I grew up very poor and suffered with abuse all my life. My whole life, I always felt that I was never wanted. I always felt that nobody loved me, and I never fit in or belonged. I did have two beautiful children that I loved with all my heart. I always tried to do what was best, but things never worked out the way I wanted them to. I don't remember anything good in my life. It was confusing, unstable, and very dark. Nothing ever went right and whatever could go wrong would go wrong. Things would happen to me and I could never understand why. I couldn't figure out why these stupid things always happened to me. I always knew I was lost. I've been lost most of my adult life. I've seen some very bad things in my life- like drinking, drugs, and sex. But at that time, I didn't know how bad I was lost. I wouldn't wish that path on anyone. I don't really know when I met Jesus. But I do know Jesus has always been with me. I know that is why I am still alive. Jesus has been walking with me. I grew up in the church. As I got older, church was not what I wanted. It seemed cold. I have been in and out of my current church, Jubilee Worship Center, for quite some time. What I love so much about this church is the love and warmth. As I finish my story, I realize that I am in a comfort zone. I do want to go ahead with God. God has brought peace in my life and joy. I'm looking forward to serving God for the rest of my life. I pray for my son and his family that one day they will come to know Jesus. I will keep praying for him, for myself,

92

and for you.

My life was like Murphy's Law; "anything that can go wrong will go wrong." It was like that until I asked Jesus to forgive me of my sins and come into my heart to lead me and guide me the rest of my life.

— *Patty*

CHAPTER 35
My Wake-Up Call

My wake-up call did not come at 6:00 in the morning, and it did not come by phone... It came at 3:00 in the afternoon as I drove my truck head-on into an oncoming truck. Have you received your wake-up call? Well let me tell you how I got mine...

I was raised in church, yet I strayed away and was running from everything I knew that was right. I had turned to alcohol to try and forget what was right. This would work for a short time, but the feelings of guilt would come back even stronger. A couple of car accidents finally grabbed my attention.

I knew what was right, and that is what I needed to get back to!! On July 4, 1991, we started drinking around the pool at 9:00 am. At about 3:00 pm, I decided to head to a friend's house to watch fireworks that evening. I never made it to his house that day. On my way there, I hit another truck head on. It spun my truck into a concrete barrier. My truck was messed up pretty bad, but I was fine. The police officer on the scene never did check me for anything. Due to God's hand, nobody had to get hurt on this day. This was the wake-up call that I needed. At that point, I decided there was one thing that had to be done.

I turned my life back to Christ and started looking for a church where I could grow spiritually. It was two months later that I ran into Pastor Combs, and I decided that Jubilee Worship Center was that place! Eleven years later, it is still my spiritual home. Praise God! If you are ready to answer your wake-up call, cry out to God today and ask Him to help you.

— *Kevin*

94

Judgement Day

The Bible promises us a final judgement:

And I saw a great white throne and the one who sat upon it, from whose face the earth and sky fled away, but they found no place to hide. I saw the dead, great and small, standing before God; and The Books were opened, including the Book of Life. And the dead were judged according to the things written in The Books, each according to the deeds he had done. The oceans surrendered the bodies buried in them; and the earth and the underworld gave up the dead in them. Each was judged according to his deeds. This is the Second Death—the Lake of Fire. And if anyone's name was not found recorded in the Book of Life, he was thrown into the Lake of Fire.

Revelation 20:11-5

At the judgement, books are opened. The Books contain every good or bad deed of every person. The book of Life contains the names of those who have put their trust in Christ to save them.

When God judges you, you will be found guilty or innocent? Will you spend eternity (forever) in Heaven or Hell?

To read more "Real Life Stories", go to the next page. For the next truth; skip to page 110.

CHAPTER 36
What Do I Have To Live For?

What do I have to live for? Who really cares about ME? Where is the positive example that I am supposed to learn from?

My life, I thought, was always pretty simple. I grew up going to church and I honor my parents for raising me in church, although their relationship didn't always reflect the Christian life. I cannot remember many details in my younger years as most people can, and still do not understand why sometimes. I do remember all the arguing, fighting, threatening, and disrespect that went on in my home. I remember many nights not even sleeping at all because of the intense arguing. Many times I remember standing in the middle of my parents all night long, crying out to them to stop, and keeping them from literally killing each other. I tried to run away many times. I always came back quickly, though, because I loved my parents so much, I couldn't stand to think that something might happen. I thought, "If I'm not there, who is going to stop them from hurting each other?" I witnessed an attempted suicide and remember so clearly the emotional impact that had on me at the time. I remember many times the police were called and I was so embarrassed for my parents' actions. They didn't seem to care about the effect it would have on their kids.

I never had any friends over at my house because no one ever cared about how our house looked or was kept up. There were rooms in my house that I had never even seen before. I think I had the neatest room in the house all the time. I had 2 older brothers and 2 older sisters, but they had the opportunity to have friends over because things weren't as bad in the house then. To my understanding, my parents always had problems that my older brothers and sisters had to deal with, but never to the magnitude that it became when I was in my teen years.

Well, thank God I never got involved in drugs or alcohol, although I did hang around friends that did. I always went to church and had a passion for music. I began playing the drums when I was 8, and played in some pretty heavy rock bands as I got older in high school. My friends lived for getting wasted on alcohol and/or drugs and having sex with as many 'chicks' as they could. I began dating a lot and having a lot of sex. It was the thing to do, and once you start, it's really difficult to just stop. I didn't think about consequences when I was with my friends. When I was alone, though, I knew what was right and wrong in my life. Many times I didn't seem to care about my life. I considered suicide many times. I thought, "Well, my parents hate each other, it seems that they hate me, I'm sleeping with girls that don't really care about me or my life. What do I have to live for? Who really cares about ME!"

My siblings had many problems in their lives as a result of the lack of positive examples. I, on the other hand, held on to one thing that I learned from the consistency of going to church. GOD CARES AND LOVES YOU WHEN IT SEEMS THAT NO ONE ELSE DOES! It always seemed that, no matter what I did or where I was, God was always there giving me a choice. He always seemed to provide a path of escape, but it was always up to me to choose and follow that path. Sometimes I chose the wrong path, but most of the time I chose to take the right path. I have seen in my family's life what happens when you choose the wrong path. I don't want that in my life!!!! I learned that in every situation you have a choice to make. You can allow that situation to mirror those same problems in your own life or you can allow it to make you a better person and learn from other people's mistakes.

Well, one of those times that God gave me a path of escape was when I was playing in a heavy metal band. I had long bushy hair and one of those jean jackets with all kinds of pins and patches on it of all the bands that became my 'idols' (it was the trend then….really!) I was dating a girl at the time that had an uncle that sang in a Southern Gospel group and they were looking for a drummer. My girlfriend mentioned this to me and I was still going to church and knew of that style of music. I agreed to meet with them and check it out. Now picture this, a southern gospel group interested in a heavy metal drummer with long hair and a longhaired heavy metal drummer interested in playing for a southern gospel group! It sounds crazy, but I now see God in that part of my life. Well, they wanted me to try out with them and I accepted. I began playing for them and continued to for about 7 years and went on to record in Nashville, two successful projects. It kept me in God's righteous path. God knew my passion at the time. He knew what excited me and made me happy.

After that, I pretty much stayed on that path. I continued to play the drums on the church praise team, got involved in Youth Ministry at my church and worked hard. I knew that although my childhood wasn't what I had wished it to be, I am in charge of my life now. The choices that I make determine my future. I had always felt the tug of God in my life to be what He wants me to be, yet I never really gave it all to Him. The routine of going to church helped me stay on the right path, but that wasn't what was the most important. The most important thing was my RELATIONSHIP with God and what I did outside of church. What I was doing in my everyday life, my consistency, my attitude, my outlook, my INTEGRITY! What you do behind closed doors where nobody sees is what matters the most to God. I began living my life that way. No, I'm still not perfect. I still make mistakes, but when I gave my life to Jesus Christ and allowed Him to have HIS way in my life, He began to guide my life in every way. I still go through sorrows and hard times, but I know that God is right there with me. I know that He will bring me out of it as long as I continue to trust in Him and live according to His ways.

In 1995, I met the woman of my dreams and married her only 6 months later. We now have four wonderful, healthy children. I love my life and my family. We have a healthy relationship. It's not perfect. We fail, but we hold on to the promises of God. I have been so abundantly blessed with a profitable business that God is now using, to allow my wife and I to be involved in ministry at our church. We attend a great church and surround our lives with positive influences.

The pleasures in this world are nothing like the pleasures of God. You can't even compare them. When you give your life TOTALLY to Jesus Christ, you receive a hope and a future that brings forth a joy in your life that cannot be replaced by anything in this world. You can't even begin to imagine the joy I have now, unless you have taken the first step in giving your life over to Jesus Christ! He is the only one that can fill your life with the joy that He created us to have! God is the One that created us in His image. He breathed the breath of life into us when we were born! He put into every one of us an empty spot that must be filled by Him in order to receive that joy! Nothing that happens in your life is too terrible that God can't turn it around and give you hope and joy in this life! You have to decide to take that right path that leads to God, no matter where you are at right now.

God will not force you to take that path, nor will He send a bolt of lightning down from the sky to show you a sign that He is real. You must have faith to believe that HE IS REAL and take the first step for yourself, then you will begin to see the blessings in your life.

If what you just read touched you in some way, that is the power of God trying to give you the hope that I was writing about. He can give you that hope right now if you take the first step in believing on Jesus Christ, confessing that you are a sinner (we all are), and that Jesus Christ died on a cross for our sins to forgive us of our sins. Then begin living a life that is pleasing and acceptable to Him.

— *Tim*

CHAPTER 37
All I Wanted Was A Family

All I wanted was a family. My husband's drunken friends were more important to him than his family. Today, I have a family, and I owe it all to...

I grew up in a broken home where no one had anything nice to say. Everything was negative. It was an abusive family, if you want to call it a "family." Since I was brought up in a broken and abusive home, I began searching for a family not like my own.

At fifteen years old, I got pregnant and had a son. I graduated from school, and I married my baby's father. We had two more children.

I thought now that I had a "family," I was set. However, that was not the case. My husband's drunken friends were more important to him than his family.

I started going to college, working a job, and trying to manage with a husband, children, and house. My marriage began falling apart, and when I couldn't take it anymore, I left.

Now, I was raising three children, going to college, and working two jobs in order to provide for all of us. All I wanted was a family—a mother, a father, and children that would do things together, have love, and communicate. I was out there looking for all that, but I didn't have it. I had my children, but I was missing a complete family.

I was also doing things that I shouldn't have been doing. Finally, I met someone and started living with him. I felt that I had the "family" that I was looking for, but there was still something missing in my life.

It was Christ. He wanted to be a part of my life. I asked Christ to come into my life, and He changed me. He wasn't just a part of my family, He became my life.

Now, not only do I have a husband, but I also have the closeness to my children, the love, the communication, and other family I longed for.

I owe it all to Jesus Christ because I let Him be the head of my family.

Are you missing a family? Let Christ into your life, and He will give you all the family you want. God has blessed me with lots of family members.

Today, I want to invite you to be a part of my family. If you are the victim of an abusive, negative, broken family or relationship, call out for help today. Jesus Christ wants you to be a part of His family. He's the best friend you could ever have. Allow Him to heal your whole heart right now.

— *Lois*

101

CHAPTER 38
Do You Need
A Lifestyle Change?

Do you need a lifestyle change? I did... I was living a life centered around drugs and work. All this changed when I met a man that is very strict when it comes to the things of God.

God used him to help me see what is really important. I have accepted Jesus Christ as my savior and my lifestyle has completely changed.

It's not always easy living a Christian life, but I'm doing the best that I can. I read the Bible. I pray. I attend church.

I am so thankful for the Godly man God has placed in my life. Friend, do you need a lifestyle change?

— *Iris*

CHAPTER 39

Where Is Love?

Where is love? It seemed as though I had nothing in my life that was permanent. Now I have only one goal in life, and that is to...

I was born the youngest of six siblings to a family with the generational curse of alcohol. My father was an alcoholic of the worst kind. My mother found Christ as a result of the abusive life that she lived in. We lived in both a physically and mentally abusive environment. Many nights I could not sleep through the night knowing that at any time my father could enter the home and "all hell" would break lose. He would beat my mother mercilessly while six children stood helplessly around and watched him beat her and had no way to help. She was the only person in the world who loved us and gave us a sense of stability. Our family was totally dysfunctional because of the situation.

Eventually with the help of God, my mother was finally able to get the courage to leave my father. I was only two years old at the time. My mother raised six children on her own. God truly was the reason for living. We had little to no earthly possessions and yet we were so happy with life.

At a very young age, I was molested. This left a horrible scar on my life that I would not realize the full extent of until I became older. I always felt dirty and never worthy of God. It seemed as though it was something that I had caused. But God helped me to fully understand and have only love for the person that caused this offense on my life.

At the age of 13, I was selected to play a lead role in a countywide production of the Broadway Musical "Oliver Twist." I sang the lead song "Where is Love?" I had no clue at the time how that song would truly describe my life.

At the age of 27, I married the girl that I thought loved me for who I was. I thought that I had truly found someone to share my life with. But, to my surprise, she later walked out and abandoned me. My trust in people was destroyed. Now the song, "Where is Love?" was more than just a tune that I had memorized; it was a true reality.

Within a one-year period, I experienced:

A divorce, a failed marriage and relationship of 18 years

The loss of a job of 13 years when the company closed its doors

The death of my father

Being forced to move because of the divorce and the inability to stay in my current home

It seemed as though I had nothing in my life that was permanent. Being raised in a Christian home, I knew all the right answers to give to someone, but now it had affected my life. I began to cry out to the Lord for help. I told the Lord that I WAS DESPERATE! He heard my cry.

As a result of the divorce, I began to devote more of my time and life to prayer and the study of the Word of God. This began to change my life. I have come to know Christ in a personal way I never thought possible. I know Christ in a fullness that I never thought could be. I am an individual that God has given many talents to, and I am a high achiever. With these talents and gifts come many hurdles. But through God, I have overcome the hurdles and have grown in the Lord and in His grace.

Now I have one goal in life, and that is to please God and put Him first. It is a daily walk with Christ. Some days are great, and some days are full of trials. But with His help, I will make it! He truly is my reason for living. If you are like me and are searching for love, you can find it all in Jesus Christ. He has promised that He will never leave us or forsake us. He said that He would be with me to the very end. He has created the stability that my life needed so much. I would not want to live without Him, and you shouldn't either. Call out to Him right now!

— *Scott*

104

CHAPTER 40
"Please Don't Shoot My Son"

"Oh, God, please don't let them shoot my son" was my thought as the voice on the other end of the phone said, "I'm sorry to be the one to tell you, but your son ran from the courtroom a few minutes ago, and the police are searching for him."

Fear gripped my heart as I asked God, "What is it going to take for my son to give his life to You?" Then, when I was told the police had him and he was safe, peace flooded my heart, and God gently spoke and told me He was still in control.

If this situation would have taken place a few years earlier, I would have panicked and been filled with fear and anger. But over the past few years, God has taken me from a broken spirit to a life filled with joy in the midst of a dark storm.

My son is 21 years old and has been in jail for eight months for the second time in two years. He spent most of his teenage years in jail, Juvenile Detention, and on house arrest because of the effects of drugs in his life. He has spent two birthdays and two Christmases away from his family and two year old son, who has yet to spend his own birthday or Christmas with his father.

My heart has been broken over my son, but because of a life-changing decision, I have peace that others cannot understand. I was twelve years old when I asked Christ to live in my heart. I was raised in church all my life, but I never truly had a personal relationship with Him. We didn't talk on a daily basis and I didn't allow God to speak to my life through His Word. Through this disobedience, I suffered from so much hurt, broken-heartedness, and disappointment. But one day God got me to pay attention, and things haven't been the same since. My life is now filled with peace and joy. I am patiently and anxiously waiting to see what God has planned for my son's life. The devil has tried to destroy us both, but God is so much greater. He has a plan of success for our lives.

— *Audrey*

CHAPTER 41

Who Has The Final Answer?

Who has the final answer? Are incurable diseases always incurable? Is the doctor's diagnosis <u>always</u> the final word? NO! There is a higher authority.

In 1995, I was diagnosed with an incurable disease (Minier's Disease). The doctor said I would be on medication for the rest of my life. He also said I would have to wear patches behind my ear. One patch only lasted 24 hours! The medication was extremely expensive. At that time, I was a widow raising 4 children. I said, "My God, how can I do this?"

Then I began to pray and ask the Lord for healing. During a revival, the evangelist asked for people to come forward and be healed. I went forward and God healed me instantly. To this day, I have never had another attack of that terrible disease.

In order to be saved, you need to tell the Lord that you are sorry for your sins and ask him to forgive you and come into your heart. Then promise to serve him for the rest of your life. Jesus wants to care for you and supply your needs.

Friend, if you have a need today, God is your only hope. Allow God to help by receiving his son Jesus Christ as your Savior and Healer today.

— *Mary*

CHAPTER 42

The
Marijuana Test

The marijuana test. When the joint comes to me, what should I do? I grew up in a nice Christian home. We went to church pretty much whenever the doors were open for services. I was taught from the start, "Stay away from drugs and alcohol." I heard it from my parents, I heard it from the Sunday School teacher, I heard it from the Pastor, and I heard it from the teachers at school.

Many of life's tests come to us when we are teenagers. The test I'm talking about now is the "Marijuana Test." Some of the neighborhood guys and I were just hanging out. They were the guys I played sports with, camped out with, and made forts with. We were all pretty much like family. We were all in a circle just talking and having a good time. One of the guys took out a joint and lit it. By this time, I knew they were all into smoking pot, but this was the first time they had ever done it in front of me. "Hey, this is some good stuff. It came from Mexico. You guys want some?" the first guy said. All the other guys said, "Yeah, bring it on friend."

I didn't say anything. When it came to me, I didn't know what to do. I sat there thinking, "Should I smoke it? Should I just suck it into my mouth and not inhale? Should I just tell the guys that I have to go home now?"

The second guy in the circle took the joint, put it up to his lips, took a big hit, held it in for as long as he could, then exhaled. "Dude, this is good stuff," he said. The joint was getting closer and closer to me. The third guy went. The fourth, fifth, and sixth guys went.

Then the big moment came. The joint was passed to me. By that time, I was very nervous. I took the joint from my friend, held it between my forefinger and thumb, and passed it in front of me to the next guy. "Wow, that wasn't hard," I thought. The guys made fun of me and said a few remarks, but I passed the "Marijuana Test."

Now, when I talk to those guys, they still say to me, "I wish I could have been like you and said 'No.' I really respect you for what you believe."

I am far from perfect. I have made mistakes, but I have been able to stay away from some very bad things in life. I have been able to say "No" and to stay away from trouble because of my parents, church, and most importantly because of Jesus Christ. I accepted Jesus into my heart when I was a young boy. It doesn't matter what age you are, what kind of things you have done, or who you have hurt. Jesus Christ will accept you the way you are. "For all have sinned and come short of the glory of God." —Romans 3:23.

It's simple. Talk to Jesus. Tell Him you are sorry for the sins you have committed. Ask Him to come and live in your heart and be your personal savior. Do it now.

— *Russ*

Standing on the Fence

I was standing on a fence and there was an incredibly large group of people assembled around it.

On one side of the group stood a man, Jesus. On the other side of the group stood another man, Satan. Separating them, running through the group was the fence I was standing on.

Both Jesus and Satan began calling to the people in the group and, one by one, each having made up his or her mind, each went to either Jesus or Satan.

This kept going on, and eventually Jesus had gathered around him a group of people from the larger crowds, as did Satan. But I joined neither group. I stood on the fence. Then Jesus and his people left and disappeared. So too did Satan and his people.

And I was left alone standing on the fence.

As I stood there, Satan came back, and appeared to be looking for something that he'd lost. I said, "Have you lost something?"

Satan looked straight at me and replied, "No, there you are. Come with me."

"But," I said, "I stood on the fence. I chose neither you nor Him."

"That's okay," said Satan. "I own the fence." "You belong to me."

You may go to the next page for more "Real Life Stories", or skip to page 126 for more truth.

110

CHAPTER 43
Have You Reached The Age of Accountability?

Have you reached the age of accountability? Is someone keeping a record of everything that you are doing with your life? Kids have a way of relaxing and feeling secure in God, however, the majority of aged Christians don't experience this security. I remember when I first heard about the "Age of Accountability." At that time, according to what I had heard, God didn't hold me responsible for any sin that I had committed. I was relaxed and didn't worry too much, at that time, about the devil getting me.

The problem is: All good things come to an end. An old Baptist Preacher told a bunch of us kids one Sunday morning in my Sunday School that 12 years old is the "Age of Accountability." He told us, "Once you guys turn 12, God begins keeping a record of you. He writes down and remembers every sin and every bad or evil thing you do from then on."

I have no idea how he came up with the age of 12. I personally can not give you a specific age, but I can tell you this; you will know when you sin.

I remember it like it was yesterday; when I turned 12, those words "God is keeping a record" stayed with me.

For years, I was up and down with God. Then finally on May 11, 1962, I prayed my most sincere prayer of repentance. From that day forward, I put forth an honest effort to serve God faithfully. Occasionally, I repeat that prayer. I have every intention of maintaining an acceptable record in the eyes of God.

There is nothing I have found that is as relaxing or that gives me a feeling of eternal security like my relationship with God. It is worth every effort you put forth.

I don't have a testimony of a life of drugs because I didn't do drugs. I wasn't involved in crime either. However, I did drink my share of alcohol, and God forgave me. I realized at an early age I needed God in my life. I asked Him to forgive me and come into my life, and He did. I have never regretted it for even one moment.

Friend, I can't give you an exact age that accountability takes place, but I can tell you that every person will be accountable before God. The only way to stand before Him with a clean slate is through His Son Jesus Christ.

— *Bobby*

112

CHAPTER 44
Why Am I Even Alive?

What is the purpose for me being on this planet? Why am I alive? Have you ever asked yourself these questions? WHY AM I EVEN ALIVE?

For many years I had often questioned my purpose for being on this planet. What am I really here for? Life is so hard. I was raised in a Christian home with biblical values. I still did not comprehend a reason for being. I had great dreams, but I lacked the stability, maturity, and faith to understand that God truly has created each person with a plan. I was told the wondrous story of Jesus and His love. I accepted Christ into my heart at a young age, yet, I could not comprehend His love for me. I found comfort in prayer. How precious and refreshing is the touch of Holy Spirit. Thank God, He always called me back. Living life was more than my mind and heart could bear at times. I faced so many sorrows.

Abuse, illness, rejection, cult-like experiences, and infertility left me in a state of depression and fear. In self-pity, I battled suicidal thoughts. I felt like I was in a deep dark pit. I was afraid of relationships. I was afraid of living life.... I longed to have purpose. I would try something for a while, but I would eventually just give up.

A family tragedy left me so wounded only God could bring me out.

My spirit was finally ready. He sent His word. I learned that self-pity was pride. I needed to be thankful that Christ had brought me through every trial. His word set me free. He came to reconcile us back to Himself.

Do I still have struggles? Yes, but I don't stay in the darkness of self pity any more. I know there's a better way to live. Corrie Ten Boom, who survived a Nazi concentration camp declares, "There is no pit so deep that God is not deeper still." I know that to be true. Jesus shined His light into the darkness of my life and set me free... Thank you my blessed Lord.

Won't you come? Christ is waiting...Yes! You were created for a purpose. Yes! There is a reason for your life. God created you to have fellowship with Him.

— *Becky*

114

CHAPTER 45
Do You Have Everything?...

Do you have everything, but still feel something is missing in your life?

I had said yes to Jesus being Lord and Master of my life at age 10 or 11, and a baptismal service soon followed. Immediately coming up out of the water, I had a feeling come over me. Since it was a comforting, good feeling, I just kept it to myself and thought it must happen to all who are baptized in water.

My teenage years seemed normal—no big rebellion (for what?). For as long as I could remember, during Vacation Bible School, a dear older woman went everyday to each class for a ten minute teaching of what the Bible said about drinking alcohol. We also had a neighbor that had difficulty getting home sometimes because of his drinking. His wife would come for my dad's help because the man had fallen over the hill and could not get up on his own. God helped me see at an early age that obeying Him was better than drinking alcohol.

One month before I was 20, Les and I were married and moved to Indiana, 400 miles away from my family and church. I thought my life would be a continuation of what I had growing up, loving my husband, raising a family, and serving God through my church work.

In the 70's, I had a comfortable home, a loving husband, and four beautiful children. I was active in Church and a Bible Study group. However, I felt there was something missing in my life, and I began to doubt if I really was a Christian. I knew God had done His part, but I questioned whether I really understood what I was doing at 10 or 11. This torment went on for about a year, and I never told anyone else what I was going through.

Then, I was given a book to read, *The Baptism with the Holy Spirit* by R.A. Torrey. My husband was gone, my children were in bed for the night, and I was doing the laundry. I was so grateful for all that I had and I began to thank God for it all. Then I began to tell Him why I loved Him. Without expecting anything, because I had only read a couple of chapters in the book, suddenly I felt love being poured into me (like after my baptism but much, much, much more). Romans 8:16 says, "The Spirit Himself bears witness with our spirit that we are children of God." That verse truly came alive in me that night, and I have never doubted my salvation again. I awoke the next morning with peace. I also had an excited hunger for the Word of God and was filled with love. The grass and trees even looked greener. I called a company to order a music tape, and they answered the phone by saying, "Praise the Lord." I felt I was going to burst inside with joy when I heard this, and I said "Yes, oh yes. Praise the Lord."

The Baptism with the Holy Spirit is to equip us for service, but the "feelings" are a side benefit.

My daughter had allergies and got shots once a week. One night I prayed for her healing. The next morning she woke up healed and never had another shot.

I went to a ladies luncheon and was introduced to a young lady that had recently given her life to Jesus. I hugged her, and she began to cry. She explained that she had been abused most of her life, and with that hug she said she actually felt love for the first time.

One day in Church, I felt prompted by the Holy Spirit to have healing prayer for a friend who had a large wart on her thumb. Nothing happened that night, but sometime during the next week or two, she suddenly realized the wart was completely gone. All Praise to God!

Perhaps you are missing the close relationship you once had with God. It may be because you let the world back into your life. I read a Christian testimony book of how an evil person came to know Jesus as Savior. This book was too descriptive of the gruesome life this person had lived. I began to feel depressed and could not feel God's presence as I had before reading this book. I had to read only God's Word and nothing else for awhile until my mind was washed clean again. We truly need the Word and the Spirit.

Whatever is missing in your life, Jesus is the answer.

— *Kay*

CHAPTER 46
Hurt By
The Church!

Hurt by the Church! I turned to the world for love, until...

When I was growing up, I always went to church. My parents took my brother, my sister, and me every Friday and twice on Sundays. As I was growing up, I never fit in. I couldn't sing or play the piano. I lived too far from the church to do the things that the youth group was doing, so they never invited my sister, my brother, or me to do anything. The only time we would be involved in anything was if they wanted something from my parents, like the many times we would have hayrides at our home.

The kids that I grew up with while attending that church would make fun of me because my parents would not let me dress like they did. As a result, I didn't want to be a part of the church or to know God because I would look at the people there, and I would see them as people who didn't love or care for others. I saw people that were just a part of a clique, which I did not want to be a part of.

When I got older, I stayed away from church. I would drink, smoke, and I did some pot and speed. I married a non-believer. He believes there is a God, but does not have anything to do with church. There was always something there that kept me from getting too deep into sin. Some call it your conscience, but I call it God. As time went by, I stopped drinking, smoking pot, and doing speed. I have been delivered from all of that for over 20 years. I have also been free from cigarettes for 10 years.

When my husband and I had our first child, I knew I had to start going back to church. I would take him Sunday mornings, thinking that that was enough. We later had two more children, and God kept drawing me to Him and talking to me. One day, about 13 years ago, I gave my life back to the Lord. At that moment, He did something that I had never felt before.

He made a change in my heart. I told Him that I would serve Him until the end of time, and that I wanted to know the real God. Not the one I saw in the people at the churches I grew up in, but to actually know Him. I asked Him to stand by my side for eternity, and He has kept that promise. I also asked Him to put me in a good church, and He did. He placed me in a church that I feel like I am a part of and where I fit in. Everything that God has done for me, He will do for you if you just ask Him to.

If you have been hurt by the church, if you turned away from God because of what people did to you, God wants to heal your hurts. Don't judge God by what people have done to hurt you. If you turned to the world looking for happiness through drugs, alcohol, and other worldly things; It's time to ask God for help! God is waiting for you. Call out to Him right now.

— *Connie*

119

CHAPTER 47

The Great Physician

The Great Physician. He did not answer my prayer. BUT HE *DID SAVE MY LIFE!*

In 1985, I was on my way home from work due to a severe pain in my stomach. I scheduled an appointment with the doctor. He scheduled a series of tests, looking for the source of the pain. All the tests results came back negative, and the doctor gave me a clean bill of health. Throughout the next two years, my body kept giving me warning signs that something was not right. As many of us do, I ignored what my body was telling me. In 1987, I again visited the doctor, but this time it was for an unrelated pain. He recommended I have surgery. I had the surgery, and after four days I was released to recover at home. During this time, the severe pain that I had experienced two years ago came back with a vengeance. The pain got to the point of being so unbearable, that my wife suggested I go to the emergency room. After several tests, I was sent home. Again, nothing was found that would cause this much pain. After three trips to the emergency room, the pain became so intense that I was literally pounding the walls with my fist desperately trying to find some relief. I began to pray like I had never prayed in my life. I threw my self on the bed and cried out "LORD YOU ARE THE CREATOR OF THIS BODY; PLEASE REMOVE THIS PAIN." God did <u>not</u> answer my desperate call. Once again I went to the emergency room. This time I went in with two pains: the physical pain and a spiritual pain deep within my heart. I always had faith that I was serving a real God, yet He was not caring for me like I had trusted. The emergency staff called my family doctor, who instructed them to proceed with admission to the hospital. During this time, the question, "Am I serving a dead God?" kept flowing through my mind. The Doctor came and gave us the news that surgery had been scheduled. He told my wife that the surgery would take, at most, twenty minutes. After

120

three hours, the doctor told my wife that my gallbladder had detached itself from my system and had developed gangrene. Part of my intestines had to be removed. The doctor said that I was lucky to be alive. For ten days I didn't eat or drink. I was being kept alive by intravenous feeding. My parents would visit me and find me in tears. They would try to encourage me, but they didn't realize that the hurt that I felt within me was that hurt that you feel when someone has let you down. I never expected that someone to be MY GOD. I was released from the hospital and began my road to a physical recovery. This young man that had placed his trust in God became doubtful, resentful, and untrusting. In other words, my faith was shaken. The days passed, and one day as I was driving home, I tuned in to a Christian radio station. A song came on, and I felt the Holy Spirit take the words of that song and drive them deep into my heart. I knew at that instant why God had not answered my call for help that day in my bed. The words of the song said, "For no one knows the sin that lies within that you refuse to share." I broke into a rejoicing cry because He was speaking to me through His Holy Spirit. Physically, God was telling me there is a rotting flesh within you that needs to be removed. It must be cut away or you will surely die physically. Spiritually, He was saying sin is the same as that gangrene. It will cause you pain and eventually take your life if it goes unchecked. No one but the Great Physician can perform spiritual surgery and cut away that rot called sin. I have learned to deeply trust Him no matter what I go through. Through my physical restoration, I have come to understand that God is also concerned about my spiritual renewal. Although I thought God did not have my best interest in mind, He showed me that He loved me and He cared enough to send His Son to the cross so that you and I don't have to die in decaying sin, but that through Him, we may have EVERLASTING LIFE.

Friend, if you have a pain in your body, whether it's physical or deep down in your heart, only The Great Physician can help you.

— *Ismael*

CHAPTER 48
I Worried
About Everything

I worried about everything. I needed something in my life. It seemed like all I knew how to do was worry. Until...

I had attended church, however I never really knew God in His fullness. I spent all my time worrying about things.

One evening, my aunt invited me to her church for a revival. I remember the preacher was really anointed and the invitation was given to receive Christ. I don't know how I got there, but when I finally got my composure back, I realized I was at the altar crying out to God.

That night, 54 years ago, was life changing. I began to take my worries to God. Immediately, relief began to flood my soul. Through prayer and studying the Bible, I found out that God wanted me to give Him all my worries. I also found out He didn't just want me to give Him all my worries, He wanted me to give Him all my needs too.

There have been some rocky times along the way. God will hear and answer our prayers, and He has been very faithful to me.

I had prayed for a good Christian husband for many years, and God sent one my way. We raised two wonderful daughters, who are in the ministry along with their husbands. We have four grandchildren, all of whom are in church and serving the Lord. I feel so blessed.

That night 54 years ago changed my life completely. I can't imagine any other way of life other than life with God. I have so many experiences of healings and miracles I could tell you about.

The wonderful life of giving your all to God will cause you to miss out on NOTHING, and I have found nothing that can compare to the way God can fill our every day. The best part is... He wants to do it for you! He is life to anyone that will accept Jesus, His son. It is so simple, and it is worth it. One day with God is greater than a thousand without Him. I would take one day and give up the thousand. It would be worth it all.

This is from my heart. My hope is that it will help you to know life can be great with Jesus in your heart. Don't hesitate to begin a great life now. You will have some setbacks along the way, but you will know and feel God right beside you every step of the way, leading you through. My prayers go out with this testimony, that you will receive this abundant life.

If you need help dealing with worry, or with anything else, call on the one that has been faithful to me for over 54 years. He will never leave you or forsake you.

— *Deloris*

CHAPTER 49
Can a Nobody
Become A Somebody?

Can a nobody become a somebody? I went from being an abused, neglected, rejected, and betrayed nobody to being a full of joy somebody. Can I tell you how?

I was raised in a small town near the Fort Bragg, North Carolina Military Base. I met and married a handsome soldier who was stationed there, and I knew we would live happily ever after. When he was discharged, we moved to Louisville, Kentucky, a much larger city. We were far away from our family and friends. By this time, we had three children and my dream of "happily ever after" began to turn into a nightmare. I discovered that my husband was an alcoholic and I became a battered and abused wife. Due to his problems with alcohol, my husband could not keep a job, and the bills went unpaid. We were evicted from many homes, and we often went without heat or food. There were times when I would knock on a stranger's door just to ask for milk for my children. I had no one to turn to, and even if I were to try, I would be beaten. The Lord always had His hand upon my life, and I knew there was a God somewhere; I just didn't know how to find him. Many times, the neighbors called the police and my husband would be arrested. I would try to hide from him, but he would always find me. The abuse became so violent that I cried out to God for help and asked Him to save me, but I had no idea what that meant. He heard my cry and sent someone who led me to Christ. Starting that day, my life changed drastically. That change has lasted for forty-seven years. I continued to cling to my marriage, and the abuse continued. But now I had someone- (God) who gave me strength, hope, and peace in the midst of it all. Going to church, we found new friends who loved us and helped us. The abuse attacks became so dangerous that my children and I were moved to Indiana by friends. These friends took us in and supplied our needs. The Lord later called me into the ministry and helped me to raise six children without any child support. So many wonderful things have taken place in my life. I was so filled with the joy of the Lord that I wanted everybody to know Jesus. I have won many to Christ, among whom were drug addicts, alcoholics, prostitutes, and even a murderer. The Lord has allowed me to preach to thousands, to travel the United States and Canada, speaking in Women's Retreats, pastoring churches, and witnessing. God gave me the opportunity to witness to millionaires, celebrities, and a governor. I had the privilege of preaching in Russia and seeing healings among the people. To God be all the glory. I was only a vessel in His hand. All things are possible with God. Whatever your need, He is the answer. For many years, I was abused, rejected, neglected, and betrayed. I was a "nobody." But Jesus made me a "somebody." I have a destiny. I have everything because of Him. What He did for me, He will do for you. Call upon Him. He will answer.

Cry out today. Call on the only one that can help you.

— *Joy*

Day Of Redemption

Jesus gave His Blood, His Life, so all your sins could be forgiven. Jesus paid your penalty for sin; in full.

Now it's up to you to accept or reject what Jesus has done for you.

If you repent for breaking God's Law and put your trust in Jesus, when God looks at you, He will not see a liar, a theif, an adulterer, or a law breaker but he will see a person that Jesus has redeemed from the curse of the Law, one that Jesus paid the full penalty for their sin. God will see the Blood of Jesus that has washed you as white as snow. Only through Jesus can you be right with God.

You may go to the next page for more "Real Life Stories" or skip to page 146 for more truth.

CHAPTER 50
I Survived
Unforgiveness

I survived unforgiveness. Now I'm full of Peace, Joy, and Love. If you would like to know how, read on...

I was born down South in a very small town. There were six children in my family: three boys and three girls. I was next to the youngest. Our family was very poor. My mom was in bad health and was sick a lot. My grandpa and grandma on my mom's side lived close by, and my grandpa grew a very big garden every summer. He helped us out a lot by giving us fresh food from the garden. I loved my grandparents very much. I think some of my best memories are of spending time at my grandparents' house. I don't remember having very many friends because we were always kept busy at home. At a very young age, my two oldest brothers and my oldest sister quit school and went to work. I remember staying at home from school a lot with my other sister to help my mother. I had a baby brother at home too. Back then, we didn't have all the modern things we have today. All of the washing was done by hand, then hung outside on a line to dry. Everything had to be ironed. It seemed like we always had work to do. I don't remember ever spending the night with friends or having friends spend the night with me. We never got to know anyone very well because we were always moving around from place to place. When I was eight or nine, we moved two thousand miles from our home to go out west. It was a very big and busy place, and it was such a change for us. The school was much bigger. We were used to going to a little country school. Being so far away from my grandparents was also very hard. Making new friends was another difficulty I faced. It wasn't long after moving out West that my nightmare began. I was a victim of childhood sexual abuse, which later turned to physical abuse. I was abused by a family member, and I didn't feel like I had anyone

I could go to or talk to. I kept it to myself and tried to pretend it never happened. I tried to forget. There was so much hurt, fear, shame, and emptiness. I had so much bitterness inside. I never did very good in school, and I didn't have any confidence or self-esteem. At the age of sixteen, I quit school. I also lost my grandpa. That year, I met a wonderful young man.

Two years later, in 1962, he became my husband. Everything that had happened to me as a child affected my marriage. I talked to my husband about the abuse that took place when I was a child; he loved me very much, but he did not know how to help me. I started smoking and would get up in the morning and smoke one cigarette after another. I tried again to put everything in the back of my mind. I tried so hard to forget. My first son was born in 1965. In 1966, I had another son. In 1967, I had a daughter. We moved to Indiana in 1971 and had another son in 1974. In 1989, I started to go to Jubilee Worship Center. I will never forget it. It was in February, and it was very cold outside. I was feeling a tug at my heart. I was not living for God. The Lord was dealing with me, so I went to church. It wasn't long after I started going to church that I knew I needed God in my life. I asked God to forgive me of my sins. That was when the heavy weight was lifted. Jesus came into my heart that night. I also was delivered of my 28 year cigarette smoking habit, but God wasn't done with me yet. I still had something to let go of—unforgiveness in my heart. I had heard many sermons about forgiveness, but it never hit me until one Sunday morning in 1994. The pastor came and asked me to evaluate his message, and I agreed to. His message was on forgiveness. For the first time, I listened. God had a reason for me to evaluate that message on that morning. That message was for me. God spoke through that message, and He said, "How can I forgive you if you won't forgive others? Forgive those who have hurt you." I realized I needed help. I did not want my adulthood to be destroyed like my childhood was. For the first time, I knew I wasn't alone anymore. I went to my pastor for help, and he prayed with me. He gave me a book to read. It was called "The Wounded Heart, Hope for Adult Victims of Childhood Sexual Abuse". My healing started through prayer and the Word of God. I asked Jesus to forgive me and to help me forgive others. God does not require perfect growth overnight. I have a wonderful pastor who took the time to help me. I had the best counselor in the world, Jesus. I now have peace, joy, and so much love for others. I don't fear anymore. I have all of this because:

1. The Lord is my shepherd, I shall not want.

2. He maketh me to lie down in green pastures. He leadeth me beside the still waters.

3. He restoreth my soul; He leadeth me in the paths of righteousness for his namesake.

4. Yea, though I walk through the Valley of the Shadow of Death, I will fear no evil; for Thou art with me; Thy rod and Thy staff they comfort me.

I am a survivor. My life has forever changed. A few months after I was saved in 1989, my husband was also saved. God is so good.

Friend, if you have been abused, mistreated, and hurt by others, don't let the past rule your future. There are some things we just can't forgive or forget on our own strength. Call out to Jesus right now. Ask Him to forgive your sins and help you to forgive those that have hurt you.

— *Pat*

CHAPTER 51
Has Fear
Controlled Your Life?

Has fear controlled your life? Has fear caused you to turn your back on the one you love? Has fear of what others may think or say about you ever stopped you from being you?

Friend, it's time for you to be who God made you to be. Do not allow fear (the devil) to hold you back any longer. I used to be bound by fear, but not any more. There was hope for me, and there is hope for you. Here's my story:

I have been going to church all my life. I first gave my heart to Jesus when I was nine years old. I was so excited. I couldn't wait to tell my teacher, Mrs. Brown. She was so happy for me.

I suddenly became afraid. Not of Mrs. Brown, but what if one of the other kids found out. What would I do? What would they think of me? This fear gripped my life. I went to church but ignored what God wanted. I let this fear come between me and God. I was shy so it was hard for me to talk to others. I had only a few friends, no one I was close enough to talk to about how I was feeling. I felt all alone and afraid.

This went on for 8 years. During this time, God would touch my heart, but I wouldn't listen to Him. But He wouldn't give up on me.

Finally, when I was 17 years old, God changed my life. He took the fear away and forgave me for turning my back on Him. He changed me. From that day forward, I have given my life to Him. He has taken away my fear! He replaced that fear with peace. I no longer feel alone!

It has been 27 years since I gave my heart to Jesus, and I haven't turned back since. If you live your life in fear, Jesus can help you. He can help you overcome your fears. If you want peace and would like to ask Jesus in your heart, just pray and believe in your heart, and He will help you too.

— *Evelyn*

CHAPTER 52

I Wanted Someone
To Love Me . . . .

I wanted someone to love me, but I was looking in all the wrong places... I was born in the state of Indiana. As a child, my family was in and out of church. When I was in the 9th grade, my mother got very sick. At that time, my life changed and things were very hard at home. By the time I was in 12th grade, I was looking for someone to love me (as a person), but I was looking in the wrong places. I ran away at age 18. A man held a knife to my throat and told me he would kill me in front of his little girl. I tried drugs and alcohol. I lived in some of the worst places you can imagine. I had cancer and went through treatment for two years. As I was going through treatment, I started looking into church with my uncle. I thought, "With all I have done, can I still be saved?" Still not able to feel loved as a person, I started looking for a family. I found a man I loved. We married thinking we would never be able to have kids because of the cancer. Yet, God gave me a little girl. I got to have my second child, which everyone also thought couldn't happen. Then, things took a turn for the worse. My husband decided to choose things other than our two miracle children and me. It was at this time I found someone who really cares. That someone is Jesus Christ. There I was with a four day old baby, a two year old child, and a husband who wanted me to help him kill himself. Jesus helped me get through that situation. With the help of Jesus I got through the divorce. Jesus has taken care of all of our needs. I have a house, healthy children, and the right people to be with. I am still cancer free and give God all the praise for that. That doesn't mean things never get rough, but it is easier knowing that... My God can do anything!!!

If you are looking for someone to love you, He does. God loves you so much that He sent His son Jesus Christ to the cross, to die for your sins. God's arms are wide open just waiting for you. Receive God's love today.

— *Christine*

CHAPTER 53
I Was Dead
On Arrival

I was dead on arrival. I heard a voice say: "Welcome home, my child." Have you found your home?

"I was born 16 years old and a mom." That's what I tell people. I was born in Georgia, but at age three, my family and I moved to Illinois. I only remember bits and pieces of my childhood. (I have the ability to forget the things I don't want to remember.) While growing up, both my parents worked. So I, being the oldest of five children, had to take on the responsibility of babysitting, housekeeping, and cooking. I was always the one to blame when things didn't go right or when my siblings didn't do things, and when they didn't do them right. My father was an alcoholic, which made my mother the strong one in our family. She was also the one who was with us most of the time. However, my mother was physically, verbally, and mentally abusive towards me, which caused me to do a lot of rebelling. I ran away from home on several occasions and was raped at the age of twelve by a slightly retarded boy who lived in our building. When I was 16 and a senior in high school, we moved to Indiana. At that time, I didn't know anyone in my class, but I soon met a boy, and we dated. I had been told that I was an embarrassment to my family, and just before I turned 18, I found out I was pregnant and became even more of a disgrace. My boyfriend and I married and had a baby boy. But I soon learned that my husband liked the wild life. He got involved with some people from the Mafia, with drugs, and with other women. At the time, I was working at the Steel Mill and had several friends who told me that I didn't need him or that kind of lifestyle. When my son was two, and I was 21, I divorced my husband. I asked God to let me keep my job until I had raised my son. He did that and so much more, yet that wasn't enough for me. Now, I was looking for something and someone to love me. I was introduced to alcohol, then drugs, men, and sex. In 1981, I was introduced to another man, and we married a year later in 1982. Soon after that, I learned that he loved to drink and party. I began drinking more, trying to keep up with him to keep peace, but that didn't work. We tried church, but neither of us was into it. We began arguing more frequently. He started beating me every time I opened my mouth, and I opened it a lot. Finally, after two years, I divorced him. By this time in my life, my father's addiction to alcohol had taken his life. He died of cancer in 1988. My father had taken care of me and my son and had become a very big part of my life. When he died, I felt as though a huge part of me had died too. My son was now 12 years old, and I learned that he was into the drug scene. I tried to stop him, but I couldn't. I fell into a deep depression, and my doctor prescribed Valium, which I later overdosed on. When I overdosed, something made me call my doctor and tell him what I had done. When I came to, he told me I was dead when I arrived at the hospital. He said I should thank God I was alive because that was the only reason I was living. When I look back over my life, I know now that God is the only reason I am alive today. After my father died in 1988, I admitted that I had a drinking problem and started to attend AA meetings. It wasn't until then that my son's problems finally caught my attention. Not only was he into drugs, he was also in trouble with the law. Everything that he had done and was doing finally surfaced. I was beside myself. I didn't know what to do or who to call. At the time, my son had been attending youth meetings at a local church. He would often tell me all about them and the people there. So, one day I talked to the youth pastor, and he told me it might help my son if I went to church. So, one Sunday evening I went. When I walked into the sanctuary, I could see people moving around and talking. But I didn't hear any noise. Then a voice spoke to me. It was a man's voice. He said, "Welcome home, my child." I looked around to see who was talking to me; no one was there, but I could hear all the noise in the sanctuary and the music playing. I let this pass. I knew from experience that alcoholics hallucinate. I sat with the only person I knew there, a friend of my son. A lady came to introduce herself to me and welcome me. They had fellowship after the service that night, and the lady invited me to join. I did. Before I went home that night, I had given her my phone numbers at home and at work. I thought that the people I had met were the nicest and friendliest people I had ever met. I felt good for the first time in a long time. She called me the next day at work and invited me to her house. I said yes. She and her children made me feel like I had

134

known them all my life. They made me feel like family. To this day, they are my family. I kept going to this church with these people who really seemed to like me and made me feel like I was a part of their lives. I wanted to belong, and I wanted what they had. I wanted to be happy like they were. I finally gave my life to God in 1988. It wasn't easy to let go of my being in control. There were times when I didn't want to go because there were things I had to give up and change. I don't like change. My son did go to jail. That was very hard for me. I blamed myself. What kind of role model had I been? I did try to teach him right from wrong, and he knew that he was doing wrong. By this time, we had a new pastor. I was comfortable enough in church now to go to him. He said he was there for us day or night. I called on him day and night. He stood by me and my son all the way. He went with me to court each time I needed him to. The first time was real hard for me. My son had never been without me. I still saw him as my little boy. On our way home the first time, God spoke to me again. I had been in church enough by now to know it was God. He put me at peace. He told me He has always been in control and always will be. All I had to do was trust Him. I thought that would be easy, but it wasn't. I still liked to take control of things. My son has been in and out of jail three times now. The last time, I made up my mind that I was going to obey God. I was going to let Him be in control. It still hurt when my son went to jail again, but God put his arms around me and held me. This time I surrendered it all to Him, and let Him take charge. I no longer felt defeated. I started really applying God's Word to my life and holding Him to His promises. Today, my son is not in jail and is trying to build a good life for himself. He is struggling, but I remind him every chance I get that he needs to let God in and let God be his pilot. While I was going through all of this, I did not face it alone. Not only did I have God; I had a church family to walk with me also. These are the greatest people on earth. I thank God every day for them. In 1989, I was introduced to a young man, who I thought was a real geek. He was much younger than me, yet he seemed much older. He helped me move one day, and we talked a lot about what he wanted. He wanted to get married and settle down. I started praying for God to send him the right girl to be his wife. One time during prayer, God spoke to me. He told me He had chosen a wife for this young man. When we didn't see who she was, I kept praying. This man and I grew to be very good friends. God spoke to me a second time while I was in prayer. He seemed to speak with more sternness. He said, "I have chosen him a bride, now go." I kept thinking, what is He talking about. In May of 1990, I married this man. We are still married today, almost 13 years later. For awhile, I was afraid of what people would think. I knew him inside and out. To me, the age difference could have meant disaster. We have both had a lot of growing to do, but we have done so with God in our lives. I don't think it would have worked without God. When I started church, I told God I wanted Him to work on me and get me right. I didn't want a man in my life unless he was chosen by God. I thank God everyday for my life, my son, my husband, and my church. I remember where I came from starting at the age of 16. I don't want to go down those same roads ever again. I promised myself that I would only follow God. HE IS MY SAVIOR! I know I am here today because even when I wasn't with God, He was with me.

Friend, today God is here for you. God can and wants to heal all of your hurts. Maybe you were raped, verbally abused, physically abused, hooked on drugs, hooked on alcohol, divorced, or have faced a number of problems and hurts. Your past really doesn't matter. From this point, it is your future that counts. God has a wonderful plan for your life. Call on Him right now, and allow Him to help you.

-- *Carolyn*

CHAPTER 54

I Lost
My Mind!

I lost my mind and I was hooked on drugs, sex, alcohol, and self pity. Until I realized there is only one way to live.

We all go through life one day at a time, not sure of what may happen the next minute. But we all have a plan for our future. Some of us call them dreams, some of us call them hopes, and some of us call them goals. I, for one, had all three of these going through my mind at one point or another in my life. Although I'm 20 years old, I already realize how fragile and hopeless we are when Jesus is not in our life.

Close to nine years ago, my parents divorced. I love my mom. She was human and I forgive her now for the divorce, but I really never understood the reason for it in my life or what goal would be achieved in it. The cause of the divorce was adultery, but I didn't know that until a month later. Even after I knew the truth, I blamed the whole thing on myself. Many harsh things were said to me by my mom, and I hated her and myself for it, but she was just as confused as I was. She didn't have Christ in her heart, but for an 11 year old boy, it really didn't cross my mind to pray about the whole thing. Dad always prayed. He even took us all to see a counselor. None of it helped because there was nothing the counselor could say to change the fact that I lost my mom, and in time, lost myself.

Months turned into years, and so we continue on with the story... I was 15 years old. My cousin introduced me and my brother Nathan to a church in Lake Station, Indiana. We were all used to the whole Pentecostal program that had to do with long skirts, flawless dress, no makeup, no piercing, no tattoos. When I first went there, I was in awe. This pastor had his stuff and he was shaking it for the Holy Spirit. I've never seen such a cooped up little sanctuary be so fired up for the Lord. I laughed at first because I thought they were all faking it. I thought they were just trying to stand out. We continued going there for a few more weeks, and I was first saved in that little cooped up church that I called my second home. My cousin taught me a lot about God. So many things about life which I really never learned because my father was lost. Not that I blame him, but after the divorce, he was never the same. None of us were. My cousin taught us how to read the Bible and how to make a habit of praying. He was never the type to tell us to do something, and then not do it himself. He would pray and read the Bible early in the morning everyday. Almost every time my brother and I stayed the night, he would talk to us about God. I think he hung out with us because God put him there as our mentor. He is more than a cousin to me. He is like a father that's really strong like "superman."

Things were good. The Lord put me through Jr. High School easily. But of course, we all go through High School blues. I met a cute girl there and ending up having a relationship with her that lasted almost five years. I began to experiment and test out new grounds that should not have been tested. Eventually, I lusted. This was the beginning of my rebellion.

After graduating from High School, I began to drink and smoke. I did it in secret because I thought if nobody knew, then it wouldn't be so bad. But it turned out to be an addiction. I was hooked for two years on alcohol, sex, drugs, and my own self pity. I began to feel sorry for myself, wondering what happened to the good old days with my cousin, always having fun without the sin. How much more exciting it was when I was a kid just to be free of sin, and thinking that drinking would some how become equivalent to that. How I used to smile all the time, and now I couldn't even flinch when the Pastor was moving in the Spirit of the Lord. Something inside me burned, but I lost touch with the Holy Spirit.

Then, I went straight. I went to the pastor to become one of his companions in an Armor Bearers class. I thought I could reach out to people who could otherwise never be reached. I was strong for awhile. I prayed and read the Bible, cut my sin completely, and sacrificed my life to the Lord as an adult, or so I thought. The devil doesn't like to see one of his little pawns go to the Lord. So he came at me with all sorts of stuff. All my past sins times 10. The devil made me think that I could do all of this and still be a servant of the Lord. "Oh, it's okay. C'mon. You're human. One slip-up won't matter."

God will always forgive you no matter what." Although these are all true except the one slip part. All sins do matter. All of your sins will catch up with you someday. I became a really hateful person. I neglected everything I learned and turned my back on God completely. I lost control of myself, and I didn't realize it until not too long ago.

In October of the year 2001, I lost my mind. I used alcohol to escape reality. I couldn't go a day without it for about seven months. I don't know what happened because I was in a drunken trance. I was lost in my own hell and thinking to myself, "Is there an escape to my life?" I became suicidal, wondering "what if" all the time. Then, I eventually got caught. I was arrested for minor consumption. I told the cop thank you, but I was still in my own trance. The cocky, arrogant, stupid me was still there, but I gave up drinking since that day. I thought God was just trying to teach me a lesson. I thought maybe He just didn't want me to go to jail over drinking. Later, as I started to get back into church, a harsh reality check hit me. This is when I became a man of God. I learned to realized that all of my sins were meaningless. They had no goal in my life. They had no hope for a future. There was no dream to be fulfilled. I know I had to go through this because the Lord knew it was going to happen. I have regrets of my past, but I can't change them. I found myself face to face with God; not physically, but spiritually. I had to make a choice. For the decisions I made before, I thought for sure that God would let the devil kill me. "Why am I even worth any of the world's air?" I thought.

But the Lord gave me another chance. He said, "You make your life what you want it to be, or you let me make your life what I want it to be." He did speak it in plain words, but I went in all sorts of directions with it. I can do this and do that and serve You and go to hell or make it to heaven with nothing in my hands to offer, or I can commit myself to You completely, taking every step of my life in faith, knowing You're going to put me where You want me to be, knowing that you will train me to be your disciple. Having the confidence that my God will speak through me when people are in need of knowledge of Him, confidence that my life will not be in vain, just as Jesus' death was not.

Life is real, death is real, faith is real, fear is real, worry is real, God is real, Jesus is real, and Judgment Day is real.

You can read this and laugh or cry. It may not have anything to do with you, or it may have substantial information that you needed to know. I have no clue what this testimony will do for you, on my part writing it was an act of discipline and obedience.

Dreaming about my life had no effect on anything. Hoping for a good future has uttered no outcome. Making goals in my life had nothing to do with my future. But by the will of God and faith in Him, He will make my life prosperous. He will reveal my destiny, and it will be so beautiful that I could never explain it. Having faith in the living God is the greatest investment you can make in yourself. You can either die for yourself and have nothing, or die for Jesus and have everything. Sounds silly? That's what I thought too, until I realized that this is the only way to live.

Friend, if you were hurt as a child like I was, Jesus wants to heal you. If you fell into the sin of the world like I did, Jesus wants to forgive and comfort you. Ask for His forgiveness, confess your sins to Him right now.

— *David*

140

CHAPTER 55
I Thought
I Was Dying!

I thought I was dying! I felt a cold chill go through my heart, and my body started to...

I was 13 years old when I started smoking pot. Pot led to PCP and acid. I was a mess at 16 years old. Then, our family moved to Ohio, where I finished school. I met a girl, and we got married and had a baby boy. We fought a lot and didn't get along well. We started swinging (husband and wife swapping), and it ended up in divorce.

I moved back to Indiana. I met a really nice girl and married her. We got along great, and she helped get me back on track. We really loved each other and were having a pretty good life together. We bought a house and truck and even some dogs. Everything seemed good.

Then, one day, I got sick and could not go to work. I went to the doctor and got medicine, but it didn't help. I thought I was going to die. I had a fever and could not breath. I had already been out of work a week. So, I laid down in my bed, closed my eyes, folded my hands together, and asked Jesus to come to me.

All of a sudden, a cold chill pierced my heart. It was like ice on my heart, and my body started to sweat. I felt a tingling all over my body. And then, I was healed. I couldn't stay in bed. I had to stand up. It felt like I had to put my hands up in the air and go to the highest place and scream, "I love you and thank You Jesus. Thank you Jesus."

I know I was healed and saved by the grace of God. Not even my faith came from me, but from God. It felt like I was in love with the whole world and wanted to bless the whole world. The touch of Jesus filled me and the whole room. I was excited.

The next morning, I got up and threw away my pot, papers, PCP's, and porn tapes and magazines. I noticed that I quit cussing and looking at women in the wrong way. I felt I had to tell everyone about Jesus and what He had done. He healed me and saved me from hell, where I was headed. If you ever need someone, call on Jesus. He is always there, and He loves you. He can't wait for you to call on Him.

— *Gary*

CHAPTER 56
I Was Mad At The World!

I was mad at the world. I heard a voice say, "I will not call you much longer. If you keep ignoring me, there will be no time left for you."

There was a time when I was mad at the world and ready to give up. I had nothing to believe in. I was lost in this world, and felt I had nowhere to turn. I was out in the streets doing things that had no purpose. Often I would reflect on my upbringing, and say to myself, "How could this happen to me?" I had a mother and grandmother who loved me very much, and tried to live as good examples... what happened to me? I'm grown now and have a family, but I wasn't always there for them. Physically I was around, but mentally I couldn't keep it together. Getting high and drunk all the time didn't help much either. Drugs had me all messed up in bondage. I almost lost my wife, kids, and job. I was a wreck. I felt like I wasn't loved, wanted, or needed. I had a family who loved me and supported me, but I was bound by drugs and alcohol and did not see all of this until it was almost to late... Then one day I had a life changing event come to my life. There was a rebirth in my life.

That rebirth came March 29, 1998. It was one of those cold wet Midwest days. Gray clouds covered the sky, and the clouds seemed to be falling closer and closer to the earth. That day, like every other day, seemed like a good day to get high or drunk to me. Except on this day God had a different plan for my life. I got dressed that morning and called a few of my friends, I didn't feel like being alone that day. Besides, if I were to get high alone I would be considered an addict. My friends came over and we had ourselves what we called a smoke session. We all smoked that afternoon, and that evening. This was all pretty routine for me. That evening we met up, drank a little and got stoned. I was feeling exceptionally hungry so I told my friends I was making a run for the nearest fast food restaurant to get something to eat. I was on my way when I passed a church. I had passed this church many times before. My mom took us there when we were younger.

The many times I have passed the church, I have had something I can only describe as a tug happen to my heart. The tug wasn't one that hurt, but something I felt inside my soul. It was like some kind of warning or reminder.

As I drove past the church, I felt a slight tug again, but I also experienced something I will never forget... a voice that consumed my body. The voice said, "Why do you ignore me? Don't you realize that I call you because I want you to listen to me? Know this, I will not call you much longer. If I keep being ignored, there is no time left for you." Almost immediately, I turned the car around and made my way back to the church parking lot. Just then I heard a different voice that said, "You're going to church right now? Don't you realize you just smoked a joint?" As I put my car in reverse to make my way back home, a man tapped on my car window and yelled, "Hey go ahead and park your car right where you are. They're singing the last song right now, then the preacher's going to speak." I went ahead and parked the car. I went inside and as I walked in, the song was coming to an end, and the pastor of the church was given the microphone. It seemed that a few people turned to look as I walked in. I thought maybe they could smell the weed on me, but right then one of the people that I thought was looking at me came up to me with a big smile and introduced themself. "God bless you brother, come over and sit by me. Is it your first time visiting here?" I kept to myself and found my way to the furthest seat from the front in case I needed to get out quick.

While the Pastor spoke, I heard that same voice I had heard as I passed the church continue to speak to my heart. I tried to ignore it, but it was so comforting to me. I continued to listen to the pastor as he spoke, and what I heard come from the pastor's mouth that day was life changing to me. I thought that the pastor of the church had the inside scoop on my life. At one point while he preached, I looked around to see if I recognized anyone in the church. I thought maybe someone in that church had told him about me and my life. I didn't know anyone there. Everything he said that night was happening to me, and I knew I had to change the way I was living before I destroyed myself and my family. At the moment I was feeling really alone, like there was a big hole in my heart and I could not get it filled. I also knew at that point that the voice I heard in my heart was the voice of God calling me to Him. I knew if I listened, everything would be alright. I knew the hole I felt in my heart could be filled. I knew I would not feel alone anymore. Just then, the pastor asked if there was anyone in the church that would like to ask Jesus into their heart. He added, "Jesus can fill any void!" I couldn't believe what I was hearing. Right then I knew that the pastor did have the inside scoop. He knew Jesus, and all I had to do was ask Him to be the ruler of my life.

I tried really hard to make it to the altar, so I could pray with someone. I felt weighted down, like I had heavy chains attached to my arms and legs. I closed my eyes and began to pray. I asked God for His help. I couldn't do it alone. I cried aloud and asked God to help me. I asked Jesus to live in my heart! Right then, I felt the chains that were holding me down start to break! Praise God, I felt free. The weight that held me down for so many years was gone. I was high, but now it was the Holy Ghost that engulfed me. I felt restored, revived, and renewed. I didn't feel the same way I used to.

I thank God everyday for giving me salvation. I give everything I have to God because He gave it to me first. I could never repay Him for all He has done in my life, His mercy endures forever. He is my provider. I ask Him to use me as a vessel and let me spread the good news of the second coming. I thank Jesus for restoring my wife, children, and family to me. I thank Him for taking me from the road of destruction to the road that leads to His marvelous light.

— *Junior*

145

Day Of Salvation

How do I get saved from the curse of the law? How do I get saved from being forever separated from God? How do I get saved from the Fires of Hell?

1. Admit that you have broken God's Law.
2. Ask God to forgive you.
3. Confess Jesus as the Son of God.
4. Confess that Jesus died on the cross for your sins.
5. Confess that Jesus arose from the dead.

The Bible says:

For salvation that comes from trusting Christ — which is what we preach — is already within easy reach of each of us; in fact, it is as near as our own hearts and mouths. For if you tell others with your own mouth that Jesus Christ is your Lord, and believe in your own heart that God has raised him from the dead, you will be saved. For it is by believing in his heart that a man becomes right with God; and with his mouth he tells others of his faith, confirming his salvation. For the Scriptures tell us that no one who believes in Christ will ever be disappointed. Jew and Gentile are the same in this respect; they all have the same Lord who generously gives his riches to all those who ask him for them. Anyone who calls upon the name of the Lord will be saved.

Romans 10:8-13

For more "Real Life Stories," turn to next page. To get saved, go to page 161.

CHAPTER 57
All Of A
Sudden . . .

All of a sudden . . . A boy felt a warmth in his heart. He felt new. He felt loved and accepted. He was changed forever. To find out how, read on . . .

In a time not so long ago, a boy was born. This boy was born a dirty, filthy kid. He grew up this way, filthy and dirty. As he grew up, he was never one of the popular kids in school. Kids would pick on him because he was big and overweight. He never felt accepted.

One day, this boy got a drum set. He played the drums every chance he could. He loved his drums. He got a little older, a little thinner, and better at his drums. But he still was not happy. He really hated himself. He felt like there was something missing in his life, so he tried to fill the gap.

One day, the boy was playing the drums and a bunch of people who hated him before, heard him playing. They said to the kid, "Hey, you're not too bad. You're pretty cool." Finally, he was accepted. Or so he thought. See, now that he was with the "in" crowd, he had to act like the "in" crowd acted. He had to talk and walk like them because he was afraid they would not like him if he didn't.

He started going to parties and drinking and having a good time. But he still was not happy. He looked big and tough on the outside, but there was something missing in his heart. He started to change. He began to have a dark attitude towards everything. To him, life was just a party with friends and music, because that was all he knew.

To top things off, he started sleeping with a girl he knew. But he still was not happy. He was depressed, and there were times he wanted to kill himself. He would ponder to himself, "I wonder if it would hurt."

This kid should be given an award for acting, because on the outside he was doing good. He had his parents and family fooled into thinking that he was fine. But on the inside, there was nothing but pain.

By this time, the boy had become a young man. This young man's friend invited him to go to church. He went, but nothing changed. Not even religion could fill the void in this young man's heart.

Then on one Easter Sunday, he went to church. Towards the end of the church service, he was at the altar and on his knees crying. He closed his eyes and saw a bright white light. In the light, he saw a cross, and on the cross was a man. The man was nailed there, and he was bleeding from his hands and feet. On this man's head was a crown of thorns, and there was blood all over his face. He knew who this man was. It was Jesus Christ. And all this kid could do was tell Jesus how sorry he was for the things he had done. He asked Jesus to come into his life and make him clean. And Jesus did just that! All of a sudden, the boy felt a warmth in his heart. He felt new. He felt loved and accepted. He was changed forever.

You might be saying to yourself, "How do you know all this?" "If you knew this boy, why didn't you help him?" Well, I do know this kid. The reason I never helped him is that the boy I am talking about is me. You see, when I was born, I was born with a sin stained soul, just like you. Dirty and filthy. And the only thing that can clean you is the cleansing power of Jesus Christ.

The sin in our lives makes us unacceptable to God. But God loves us too much to be away from us. So He sent His only son Jesus Christ to die for our sins. He took our place on the cross that day when it should have been me and you. He loved us so much, He gave up His life so we could live. They took His body off the cross that day and buried Him in a tomb. He was in there for three days and nights. But early Sunday morning, He arose for you and me! He's alive!! Not even the grave can hold Jesus. He is bigger than death. And now, He sits at the right hand of the Father in Heaven. He would do it all again if He had too. Even if you were the only person on earth, He still would have come and died for you. But He does not have to come and do it again because He paid for the sin of all mankind. He loves you that much!

Maybe you have done some of the things I have. Maybe you have done worse or maybe nothing at all. The fact of the matter is, without Jesus to cleanse you of the sin you were born with, you're not going to make it. Maybe you feel as if what you have done in the past is too big for God to forgive. But Jesus died for all of your sins, no matter what they are.

— *Bill*

CHAPTER 58

I Cried!

I cried! I was one that hardly ever cried, but I cried that day, and my life was changed forever...

When I was attending a Baptist church many years ago, I answered the altar call and was saved. But I did not do so because I was a sinner. I did not even know that I was a sinner. Sinners were so obvious—murderers, adulterers, fornicators, thieves, abusers of women and children—and I knew I was definitely not in that category!

If I did not know what I was being saved <u>from</u>, how could I possibly know what I was being saved <u>for</u>?

Why then did I go forward? I really didn't know. The sermon that day, while it may have been informative, was not compelling, and there was no sense of urgency in the altar call. Yet, there I was, all by myself standing at the altar.

One thing I did know was that my life was changed that day! I was one who rarely cried, but I cried that day. The further genuineness of that experience proved itself a few days later, when I suddenly discovered that my manner of speaking had gone through a tremendous change. All the expletives were just gone—trading "did you hear the one about" stories were just gone . . . I no longer wanted to smoke, and I had joy!

I still did not consider myself a sinner. I just wasn't one of "them." No one could have convinced me that I was a sinner. The good news is that God did. He very gently led me into a new realm of thinking and reasoning. Things that I never would have considered wrong were revealed to me, as He showed me that sin comprises so much more than what my version of sin had been. He showed me in such a way that there was no room for contradiction or rationalization. Yet always in a non-condemning way. So, now I knew what I was being saved <u>from</u>, but I had yet to learn what I was being saved <u>for</u>!

I knew nothing about serving or servanthood. They were just not a part of my thought process. Oh, I had heard the words about serving and servanthood, I had even sung about them. But I did not "know" them, and there's a big difference.

Again, God in His mercy, and through the preaching of the pastor, began to show me what it means to serve, and in so doing, showed me what I was being saved <u>for</u>.

I now know why I went forward that day many years ago. It was because God had pity on me. He knew how unaware I was of my true condition, and He knew I needed Him. It was all because of His mercy and grace.

Today, I stand in appreciation for all He has done for me, and I know that He is not through with me yet. I fail often in my longing to lead a consistent Christian life, but I know He will come through for me. He is the same yesterday, today, and forever.

Without Him, my life would be empty. With Him, my life is overflowing!

— *Ruby*

CHAPTER 59
My Son
Was Kidnapped

My son was kidnapped. There were times in my life when I felt like I just wanted to die...

At the age of 15, I married my first husband. He was twelve years older than I was. I married just to get out of my parents' house. My parents and my family were poor, and I did not want to be a burden.

My husband and I were married for twelve years. It was a very unhappy marriage. My husband was an excessive gambler and was never home for my son and I. I can recall one time when my son was ill, and I couldn't find my husband anywhere. My son's godfather had to take us to the hospital. When I finally found my husband, he was in another woman's house.

After twelve years of marriage, I got tired of the cheating and gambling. I left California with my son and moved back to Indiana with my family. Months later, my husband came to Indiana to try to get me back, but I told him no. A week later, my son went to the store with my sister and my niece, and my husband kidnapped my son at gunpoint. The police wouldn't do anything about it.

I worked in Illinois to pay for my divorce, and the courts gave me custody of my son. Then, I found out that my husband had taken my son to Puerto Rico to live with his aunt. I was never able to get the money to go to Puerto Rico to fight for custody of my son. I suffered a lot. It was the grace of God that got me through it all. I wasn't able to see my son until he was a grown man. He came to see me with his wife. It was a blessing that God brought my son back to me.

Years later, I met the father of my second son while I was working in Illinois. We were together for four years, but we were never married. We didn't stay together because when my son was one year old, I came home to find his father in my bed with another woman. I left and never saw him again. I never received any help from him for my son. I had to struggle and work hard to support my son and myself.

While working cleaning a house, I met my youngest son's father. We stayed together until my son was three years old. Then we separated because he was an alcoholic and was verbally abusive to me. He gave me child support, but I still struggled to take care of my two boys.

I don't regret what happened in my life. I just thank God that I was able and in good health to do what I had to do. At that time in my life, I didn't know the Lord like I know Him now. I was doing some things that I knew were wrong in God's eyes. As my sons got older, they began to hang out with the wrong people. I felt like they were headed for self-destruction, so I decided to move them away from the trouble. We were living in East Chicago, and we moved to Lake Station.

In Lake Station, I met my current husband. We went through a lot of ups and downs. At first, he was a heavy drinker and was verbally abusive. We separated for awhile, but then he changed his life around and we got back together with God's help and a lot of prayer. We are both God-fearing people now. There were times in my life when I felt like I wanted to die because I didn't know God at that time. I had done so many wrong things, and I was paying the consequences for all the things I had done.

I began to go to church with my youngest son, and that's when I met the Lord. I realize that even though I had done all those things, I met the Lord in a mighty way, and He changed my life completely. If you want to change your life, ask Him for forgiveness and to come into your life like I did.

— *Carmen*

CHAPTER 60

I Changed!

I changed! A miracle happened in my life...

At age seventeen, I called out to God desperately for ten days, "God, if you are really there, or if I have been too bad, let me know." On the tenth day, I said, "God, I believe you are there. I must have been too bad."

Later that day, a friend's father called me and said, "Lisa, for ten days, God has been telling me to call you..." I went with him to a Full Gospel Business meeting. At the end of the meeting, the preacher invited people to come up front and pray. I knew God had heard and answered my prayer, so I went and prayed. "God, I am sorry for the wrong things I have done. Please forgive me. Come into my heart and be Lord of my life."

At that moment, a miracle happened. I changed! Twenty years later, I'm still calling out to God, and He still answers me. I hope you will do like I did. Call out to God with all your heart. Don't give up. He will answer you.

— *Lisa*

CHAPTER 61
Something Fantastic Happened To Me

Something fantastic happened to me, and I want to share it with you. Please let me tell you an amazing story.

When I was 54 years old, I was bent out of shape, physically and mentally. I had arthritis so bad that I had to waddle just to walk forward. The only way I could get out of bed was to fall out and crawl to a chair and pull myself up. Mentally, I was a vegetable. I felt as if I had but six months to live. I was as low as a man could get and still be alive. I desperately needed a miracle and received it. It came when I asked Jesus into my heart and turned my life over to Him. He instantly saved my soul. Almost immediately 98% of the pain left my body. My face was wrinkle free, and I could stand up straight for the first time in many years.

Someone asked why I suddenly looked years younger. Up to the time Jesus changed me, people would remark that I was the oldest looking 54 year old man they had ever seen; that I looked more like a 90 year old.

Maybe, right now you are in pain and need a friend to talk to, someone to sympathize with you, someone to bear your burdens, someone to love you, someone who will never leave you or forsake you. If you will call out to Jesus with sincerity, He will come into your heart, renew your mind, body, soul and Spirit.

After you have called out to Jesus, start reading the Bible everyday, and pray everyday. The benefits will amaze you. You will enjoy better health and more love and compassion for others when you begin to line your life up with the Word of God. You will have all this and more than you can possibly imagine.

Romans 12:1 & 2 says, And so dear brothers, I plead with you to give your bodies to God. Let them be a living sacrifice, Holy, the kind he can accept. When you think what he has done for you, is this too much to ask? Don't copy the behavior and customs of this world, be a new and different person with all freshness in all you do and think. Then you will learn from your own experiences how His ways will really satisfy you.

I love you, but Jesus loves you even more.

-- *Ray*

CHAPTER 62
My Mother Tried To Warn Me

I was born May 28, 1938 into a Christian home. I asked Jesus into my life to be my Lord and Savior on November 12, 1950. I graduated from high school in 1957, spent two years in the Navy, and married in 1965.

My mother tried to warn me, but I would not listen. I knew better than her. I was divorced in 1975. I went out into the world to live a life of sin, alcohol, drugs, and pornography.

But God had other plans for me. One night in 1989, I had a dream that brought me back to my senses and reality. I started attending church, and on October 11, 1990, I asked Jesus to forgive me of my sins and to come into my heart and stay forever. And He really came in!

Praise God, Jesus set me free from alcohol, drugs, and pornography. He made me a new person. Now I thank the God and Father of my Lord Jesus Christ for His love and mercy and for not giving up on me. This personal relationship with the Creator of the Universe is the only thing that matters to me now, and I give God all the glory.

What He has done for me, He can and will do for you. Jesus can set you free to be all you were meant to be. Will you ask Him into your life now? He wants you to have abundant life now and in the age to come, eternal life in heaven.

-- Ed

CHAPTER 63
I Was at a Dead End

I was at a Dead End! I was depressed and empty. I did not know what was going to happen to me. Then I made a decision that changed me and brought a great peace to me.

The day I decided I needed change in my life was the day I asked Jesus to forgive me of my sins. I was raised in church. At sixteen years old, I got my first job and was introduced to the ugliness of sin. I gradually stopped going to church and felt I could control my own life. I was married at 18 years old. My mother-in-law was totally against the marriage. While pregnant with my first baby, she constantly tried to convince me to get an abortion. She knew how I could get one without having to pay for it. I repeatedly refused. She didn't want her son tied down with a family. I struggled with the fact that she wanted my baby murdered for her own selfish reasons. At 19 years old, I had a beautiful, healthy son.

After his birth, the marriage turned sour. I lived with physical and verbal abuse. My home was anything but happy. There was always turmoil. I never knew from one minute to the next if I would be hit or kicked around. I couldn't do anything right according to my husband. He would continually tell me he didn't mean what he said or did to me when he was in his violent rages. My husband was using drugs and alcohol.

At 21 years old, I felt like my life was hopeless. I was miserable and felt like I would lose my mind. I was at a dead end. I didn't have much of a work history to rely on. I was depressed and empty. If not for my son and family, I don't know what would have happened to me. My mom and church were continually praying for me.

One day in December, I was so upset about my home situation that I walked three miles to my mom's house. That day, my decision to accept Jesus as my savior changed my life. My God-spot was filled to overflowing. I had peace even though my home situation didn't change. I was a changed person.

My husband at this time was very jealous and distrustful of me. There were times I was beaten up for attending church or if I wanted to spend time with friends or family. He wanted total control of me and my life. I lived in fear of him, but I felt God's presence with me.

During the next few years, I experienced two miscarriages, which were very difficult to deal with. Again, God calmed my grief and blessed me with a complete recovery.

A few years later, I was blessed with a beautiful daughter. She was my sunshine during a very dark time in my life. I continued to hold tight to my relationship with God. Drugs, alcohol and violence continued and eventually destroyed the marriage, which ended in divorce.

God has been the friend to listen to me when I didn't make sense to anyone else. He loved me when I was unlovable and loves me just as much now. God was with us when my daughter was going through depression in elementary school, when my ex-husband threatened to kill me, my parents, and kidnap my daughter. He protected us and blessed me with a sound mind.

God has also been with me through the joyous times. I graduated from college at the age of 38, and now I'm working as an RN. I married a Christian man who loves me beyond reason. God healed my daughter of depression, and I could fill a whole book with the other ways God has blessed me.

God wants to bless you the same way and to be to you what He is to me. Instead of looking to things and people to fill your empty spot, God can and wants to. The longing you have in your heart that nothing else can fill is your God-spot. God is the only one that can fill it properly so you won't feel empty inside. Your situation may not change, but you will. God hasn't always calmed the storms of my life, but He has calmed me! He helps me get through the storms. I trust Him, really trust Him, to be my anchor that always holds no matter what.

God has blessed me more than I could ever have imagined. He will do the same for you, and it starts with asking Jesus to forgive you of your sins. God will be there to help you be strong when you're too weak to stand alone. He will give you the desires of your heart. It took a long time for my home environment to be what I longed for, but God knew my hopes and dreams of a Christian home without fear and violence.

-- Sherri

It's Time To Pray

If you have already confessed your sins and cried out to God you are saved. If you have not, its time that you do. Pray this right now:

Dear God,

I acknowledge You as the Creator of all things. I admit that I am a law breaking sinner, and I deserve the Fires of Hell. I throw myself at Your feet and ask for Your mercy and forgiveness of my sins. I believe that Jesus Christ is Your son. I believe that Jesus died on the cross for my sin and I believe that You raised Him from the dead. Jesus, please come into my heart and fill that place in my heart that belongs only to You. Jesus, I declare You Lord of my whole life today and I will confirm my salvation by telling others what You have done for me. Thank You for saving me!

For more "Real Life Stories," go to next page. To find out what to do now that you're saved, go to page 170.

CHAPTER 64
You have two weeks to two months to live

"You have two weeks to two months to live." I went into a state of shock, and my body began to jump all over the bed. My body stopped. Suddenly, a calm came over me, and....

Dear Friend, let me tell you of a life that was filled with sorrow, pain, loss, and distrust.

I saw God for the first time at the age of five. By that, I mean I saw His power at work. I witnessed many miracles, blinded eyes opened, and crippled people walk. This made a lasting impression on me. I knew that if I ever got religion that it had to be the real thing, not some form of what I knew it to be. I wanted that same God that I had read about in the Bible. This man called Jesus had to be real to me, not just someone I read about in a book.

Before I was 16 years old, I had lost my parents, brother, grandparents, aunts, and uncles. I had lost all the support systems that a teenager should have. I had no home, no family, no money, and no way to care for myself. I quit school and roamed around the country for the next two years. I was looking for replacements of what I had lost and a place to belong. I became involved with drugs, thinking that they would help me find my place in the world I had to live in. But they only succeeded in making me dependent on them.

I lived in abandoned cars and anywhere I could find a warm place to sleep. During that time, I was raped, beaten, and robbed. I wanted to die. I overdosed on drugs. As you probably realize, I did not die. Instead, I ended up in the arms of a Christian lady. When I awoke, she was praying for me. It was pretty intense. This was a person that I had previously rejected. I thought she hated me. She asked nothing of me except that I keep in touch with her.

A short time later, I found out I was pregnant. I thought this wonderful little gift would be my salvation from the horrible life that I was living. Not even then did I consider God as the answer. I married after my baby was born, but the marriage did not last. My husband was physically abusive and cruel. I suffered many beatings at the enemy's (the devil's) hands. One night, it almost became deadly. My husband came home and sat across the kitchen table from me. He pulled out a 9 mm automatic gun. It was cocked and loaded. He pointed it at me and said he was going to kill me. When I asked him why, he said that if he couldn't have me, no one could, including God. I had to make a decision, so I began to pray. My husband became outraged and hit me across the back of my neck with the gun. I fell to the floor. When I awoke, I was in the hospital with a broken neck. Again, there was the Christian woman who had prayed for me years earlier. Once again, God had protected me and my children. I could not go on like this. I needed to decide if I would stay with my husband or leave him, but I ended up not having to make that decision. He died of a massive heart attack not long afterwards. I did not know if God had anything to do with it, but the Bible says, "For every trial, He will make a way for our escape."

Later, I met a man that was a Christian, and we got married. He encouraged me to go to church with him, and I soon began to seek God's face again. But that was not the end of my troubles. Even though I had found God, my faith was to be tested again. Shortly after we were married, I was told I had cancer and that I better get someone to raise my children and make arrangements for my funeral. The doctors had given me two weeks to two months to live. That night in the hospital room, my life ran like a movie before my eyes. I thought, "God, how will my children grow up without their parents, as I did?" I went into a state of shock, and my body began to jump all over the bed. I remember trying to control it, but I couldn't. I saw a cross on the wall at the end of my bed. As I concentrated on the cross, I mouthed the words, "God, if you will heal me, I will serve you for the rest of my days." Things moved quickly from there. Suddenly, my body stopped. A calm came over me, and I slept through the entire treatment. When I awoke, my husband was sitting in a chair across from my bed, and he was crying. As I spoke to him, he lifted his eyes and thanked God. God had healed me.

When the x-rays came back, the doctor could not understand where the cancer had gone. He had both sets of x-rays in front of him. The first one showed the cancer, and the other showed no cancer at all. He asked me if I knew what had happened. I told him that God had visited me the night before in the hospital room and had touched my body and taken the cancer away. The doctor said, "I don't know if that stuff really works or not. All I know is that it was here yesterday, and today it is gone."

In three days, I went home to my husband and children with the determination that I would live for the Lord no matter what happened with my life.

Friend, if you can relate to any of my story, know one thing for sure: God is real. He will never give up on you, and He will never leave you. All you have to do is call on Him, and He will show up.

-- *Zelma*

164

CHAPTER 65
We Live in a Prideful Society

We live in a prideful society, where humbling yourself can be considered a weakness. Please read this, so I can show you how I found out that humbling yourself is really a sign of strength.

I want to tell you a story about how God delivered me from cigarette addiction. I had been a smoker for about fifteen years at the time and had tried several ways to give up the habit, all to no avail. Then a lady, we were friends with where we lived at the time, told my wife a story about her dad who had to have a lung removed after he had stopped smoking for 25 years. This scared me very badly, to think that even after quitting for 25 years, you could still lose a lung. But it seemed that no matter what I did, nothing worked, until my wife said, "Why don't we pray about it?" I said I had tried everything else, why not give God a try. Now mind you, I had been a Christian for a few years and should have thought of it myself, but sometimes we can't see the obvious (kind of like the sin in our lives). So, we prayed that my addiction would be lifted from me. I didn't feel anything right away after we had prayed, but while we were in bed I felt impressed to turn in my Bible to II Chronicles 7:14 which reads: "If My people who are called by My name will humble themselves, and pray and seek My face, and turn from their wicked ways, then I will hear from heaven, and will forgive their sin and heal their land." NKJV

When I read this verse of scripture, it hit me that I needed to pray for forgiveness of the sins that I had committed in the eyes of the Lord, and when I did this, almost immediately it felt as though a large weight was lifted from me. It was as though I could feel the addiction leaving my body, and after that day I never smoked another cigarette again. I was delivered from my addiction. And believe it or not, I never had any cravings. Everything left me.

All it took was recognizing the sin in my life and confessing it before the Lord. As the verse says, "if My people who are called by My Name," and we are all God's people. If we will humble ourselves, boy that's a hard one, isn't it, to humble yourself before anybody. We live in a very prideful society where humbling yourself can be considered weakness. I'm here to tell you that humbling yourself is not a sign of weakness. It is a sign of strength, and this is what it takes for us to humble ourselves before the Lord and pray and seek His face. Then we have to be willing to turn from our wicked ways, to confess to the Lord that we are sinners, and there is no other way but His. Praise be the Lord. The last part is the reward, because if we do the first part, then He will hear us, that is, hear our prayer, and will forgive our sin and make us whole. All we have to do is ask the Lord to forgive us and He says in His word that He is faithful to forgive us. 1 John 1:8-9 says, "If we say that we have no sin, we deceive ourselves, and the truth is not in us. If we confess our sins, He is faithful and just to forgive us our sins, and to cleanse us from all unrighteousness."

What are you dealing with today, maybe an addiction of some sort? It comes in many forms; drugs, cigarettes, alcohol, or pornography, etc. Whatever it is, I'm here to tell you that you can be "cleansed from all unrighteousness." All you need to do is call upon the Lord, humble yourself, acknowledge before the King of Kings and the Lord of Lords that, yes, you are a sinner, but you want to turn from your wicked ways and the Lord Himself tells us that He will hear from heaven (He will hear our prayer), and He will forgive us of our sin, and He will heal our land (cleanse us from all unrighteousness).

So, why not start today?

-- *Tony*

CHAPTER 66
What Do You Want to Be...

What do you want to be when you grow up? I am what I always wanted to be. How about you?

Have you ever been asked this simple question? What do you want to be when you grow up? I think that all of us at some stage in our life have pondered this. My question is somewhat similar. It demands the same amount of pondering. Many of us give up on our hopes and dreams due to unforeseen circumstances in our life. Some may always have that reoccurring thought of what life would be like if they had only done things differently, or if they would have completed college, or ever listened to well meaning parents who offered words of wisdom in given situations. You, as well as I, know that looking back with regret or in some cases even remorse, does not change our present situation. However, it may haunt a secret place in our mind and open doors that need to remain closed. Could this information be of interest to you? Then read on, my friend.

Life and adolescence for me were a wonderful experience. You are not going to read of any type of abuses or addictions. I was raised in a Christian home. However, I would like to offer a definition of the term, Christian, that is so lightly used in our day. Christian means to be like Christ. My sister and I were shielded from the evils of this world to the very best of my parents' ability. We were taken to church and encouraged to be active participants in all the activities. I never heard my parents speak disrespectfully of any of our pastors, government leaders, or school officials. They were honest and usually taken advantage of because of their generosity. My sister and I were encouraged to pursue our dreams and aspirations with much support, love, and acceptance. I did venture from the teaching of my parents for a few very short years and became acquainted with all the traps that present themselves to our young people. Thank God for praying parents and other Christians who called my name in prayer.

My heart and life were returned to Christ in 1976 while I was in the 9th grade at Edison High School. It was at that time that I began my pursuit to become what I always wanted to be. It is with much joy and appreciation that my endeavor was to be a preacher's wife. I not only wanted to serve my Lord, but also the one He called to serve His people. It is a most honorable position, one in which I feel most unworthy and not to mention inadequate. However, it is who I am and what I always wanted to be.

My life is not one of remorse, regret, or of what if's. It is one of certainty because I am certain that Jesus Christ placed me where I am today. I have peace that passes all understanding, even in times of difficulty. My past has never haunted me, and my future is destined to succeed, and carries with it a guarantee written in the blood of my risen Savior. I am what I always wanted to be, and that makes life full, complete, and happy for me. Since you are still with me this far, I am going to assume that your life may need someone to bring completeness, peace, and certainty. You may need someone to remove regrets and remorse and to answer those questions that sometimes just seem so difficult to find answers to. Questions like, "Where did I go wrong?" "How did I get off track?" "Is it too late for me?" "How can my life ever be one of peace in a world where uncertainty reigns?"

There is no answer to these questions without Christ, but through Christ and a real genuine relationship with Him, answers come, and the pieces to the puzzle of one's life begin to fit. Hope in every circumstance is renewed. Jesus is the answer, and you can be what He wants you to be, even if you are all grown up and even if you are not! It is a mysterious phenomenon that takes place. It is one that cannot be explained, but has to be experienced. He someway and somehow makes all things new and okay. One more question: What do you want to be when you grow up? A Christian or not? If you chose to be a Christian, you chose eternal life.

If I can be of any assistance to you, I am the senior pastor's wife at Jubilee Worship Center. I would love to meet you and hear about all the wonderful things Christ has done for you.

--*Lisa*

168

CHAPTER 67
I Was Lonely
And Scared

I was lonely and scared. I knew there was something very important missing in my life. But what was it?

I grew up in a good home with great parents and six older siblings. I was the youngest in our family. We were a typical middle-class family. We went to church every Sunday. Dad worked, mom was a housewife, and my siblings were all educated, successful people. I was a pretty normal child, pretty well behaved, a decent student, and involved in cheerleading and basketball.

Then, at age 11, I began to make some pretty terrible choices. My friends and I started experimenting with alcohol. We went from sneaking a beer once or twice a month to getting wasted every weekend. Sometimes we even drank before school.

One time during a party at my friend's house, my best friend and I shared an entire bottle of rum and got alcohol poisoning. We fell down the stairs, passed out, and woke up in our own vomit. That was not enough to stop us.

I got to a point when alcohol alone could no longer fill the void that I felt in my life. I began to look for other ways to fill the void. When I was 13, I threw a huge party at my parents' house. Their house got trashed, one of their cars was damaged, and there was beer all over the place. Three months later, when I got ungrounded, I got arrested for shoplifting. I continued to make poor choices. I knew right from wrong, yet I chose wrong every time. I began looking for love in all the wrong ways. I began by flirting way too much. Which, when mixed with alcohol, led to sex with guys who took advantage of me while I passed out.

So there I was, 13 years old, with a criminal record and parents who were devastated by the things their teenage daughter had done. They didn't even know the half of it. I continued to do wrong. By the time I was 16, I was in a pretty bad relationship and had also added some drug use to my list of bad decisions. The guy I was involved with was a drug dealer, arrested several times, and pretty violent. I thought I was in love, and against my parents begging and pleading, I continued to sneak around and begging my friends to take me to see him.

Then I found out I was pregnant. This was a huge wakeup call for me. I knew I had to stop being so selfish because now I was responsible for someone else's life. I stopped drinking and stopped smoking cigarettes and marijuana. I started growing up. I severed ties with my boyfriend, with my parents strong encouragement. It was at this very lonely, scary time that I knew there was something very important missing in my life, but what was it?

After the birth of my son, I got a full-time job. Through this job, I met someone who was different from all the people I had hung out with over the last 6 years. He was kind, quiet, polite, and just different. We began dating, and on our third date, he took me to church with him.

It was then that the light finally came on. That is what I had been missing. That night, I made a connection with God. I discovered that I needed a personal relationship with God instead of looking for relationships with guys or other bad influences.

God filled me with His love and changed my life from that night on. Friend, if you're lonely, if you're scared, if you have made wrong choices, if you have something missing in your life like I did... Call out for help right now. Call on the one that turned my life around. Call on Jesus.

-- *Valerie*

170

You Are A New Person

The Bible says:

When someone becomes a Christian, he becomes a brand new person inside. He is not the same any more. A new life has begun!

2 Corinthians 5:17

Say this:

I am a new person. I have a new life, a God centered life.

The Bible says:

All these new things are from God, who brought us back to Himself through what Christ Jesus did. And God has given us the privilege of urging everyone to come into His favor and be reconciled to Him.

2 Corinthians 5:18

God bridged the gap of sin between you and Him by Jesus dying on the cross. He now has given you the honor and privilege of telling people how to find that same favor with God through what Jesus has done for them.

The Bible says:

He died for all so that all who live — having received eternal life from Him — might live no longer for themselves, to please themselves, but to spend their lives pleasing Christ who died and rose again for them.

2 Corinthians 5:15

Jesus died so you could have eternal life with Him in Heaven. Jesus is calling you to now live for Him, doing only those things with your life that would please Him.

To learn more about what you should now do, go to the next page.

What Do I Do Now?

1. Find a church, and attend every time the doors are open.
2. Attend Bible studies and Sunday School.
3. Get a Bible, and read it every day.
4. Pray every day, morning, noon, and night.
5. Tell people what Jesus has done for you.
6. Write out your real life story, your testimony, and give it to people.
7. Make a public profession of your faith by being baptized in water.
8. Shout. Yes, Shout! Friend, you have something to shout about. You've been set free. Death cannot hold you, and Hell can't have you. You belong to God and no matter what happens in this life, as long as you continue to walk with Him, you will be with Him in Heaven...

Church Outreach

Every member in every local church has a real life story (a testimony).

One of the most effective ways to teach Christians how to share their faith is to get them to write out their testimony (real life story) and share it as part of their every day life style.

The "Witnessing Made Easy" series on audio cassette tape covers the topic of sharing your testimony plus many, many more effective ways to witness. For more information and resources about witnessing call, write, or email:

Step By Step Ministries
215 Sauk Trail
Valparaiso, IN 46385
219-762-7589

E-mail: Jim@step-by-step.org
website: www.step-by-step.org
website: www.theshofarman.com

172

A Word From the Pastor

Some years ago a popular television detective drama would use the phrase "The story that you are about to see is true. The names have been changed to protect the innocent." Well, I can tell you as the pastor of Jubilee Worship Center Church of God in Hobart, Indiana, the stories that you have read are true and the names have not been changed or altered in any way. They are the Real Life Stories of the people who make the wonderful congregation that I pastor.

As you may have noticed, my story is not a part of this book. It is not that I don't have a testimony or that I am too ashamed to share what my life was like before I met Christ. It is, however, my desire to allow you to read about everyday people, like yourself, to whom you could relate. So often when you hear the view of a minister, people seem to close down because they say, "Well, he's the pastor, it's expected that he would say or do that..." I want you to hear from ordinary people, not a pastor. I can tell you that the stories that you have read represent a cross section of so many in our society. People all across this nation and literally around the globe have struggles, questions, situations that they feel they feel there is no hope, and that they are the only ones to ever have an experience like theirs. The Bible expresses in 1 Peter 5:8-9 "Be sober, be vigilant; because your adversary, the devil, walks about like a roaring lion, seeking whom he may devour. Resist him, steadfast in the faith, knowing that the same sufferings are experienced by your brotherhood in the world." (NKJV) We are not the only ones that are experiencing that particular struggle, crisis, temptation or trial. There is someone who is either going through the same thing at the same moment or there has been someone who has gone through what we are going through. That is why I feel it so vital that you read this book and pass it on to someone else.

How interesting it is to see how relevant the Bible and the church can be, even in this century. How many times I have heard people say to me, "I can't get any thing out of that book!" or "I go to church, but I come away the same way I went in." For many, these are true statements. However, it is not so for many of the people who come through the doors of Jubilee and the "Real Life Stories" prove this!

You may have noticed how direct and confrontational some of the chapters are. They are that way for a reason. So many times, people misunderstand God. In our western culture we are told that we are to be "politically correct" and not to rub people the wrong way because they will not listen or read what you have to say. They say that God is a loving God and He loves everybody so you have to be non-intrusive with the gospel. This is only a partial truth. While God is a Loving God and Father, we cannot forget that He is a just God as well. He is a God that is to be feared. Not to be scared of, but to be revered and honored. How true. However, God gave us grace so we would walk in obedience to Him. In Hebrews 12:28-29 we read "Wherefore we, receiving a kingdom which cannot be moved, let us have grace, whereby we may serve God acceptably with reverence and godly fear: For our God is a consuming fire." All one has to do is read the book of Revelation to see that God is the Judge of the whole earth and if one does not come to Him as the Lamb that takes away the sins of the world, they will have to stand before Him as the Lion of Judah, the Judge of all creation.

It is not our intent to water down the message of salvation. Nor is it our intent to be offensive. However, it is our intent to be painfully honest with the readers. You need to hear the truth. God's word tells us in John 8:32 the Truth will make you free. It also states that "God's word is living and active. It is sharper than any two-edged sword and cuts as deep as the place where soul and spirit meet, the place where joints and marrow meet. God's word judges a person's thoughts and intentions." (Hebrews 4:12 God's Word Version) Because God's word is a living book, the truths contained in it will enable you to walk in obedience to God's commands. A person does not have the ability just within himself to do so. If they did, Christ would not have had to give His life to free us from the bondages of sin. All I ask that you do is consider the Real Life Story of Jesus found in the Bible. You will see that He came so people like you and I could finally be free. Free from sin. Free from shame. Free from addictions. Free from guilt. Free from pain.

We at Jubilee Worship Center believe that God can give everyone a "New Beginning." Are you one of them? If so, I want to encourage you to take a moment and reflect on what you have read and simply ask God to give you a "New Beginning." It is as simple as ABC. <u>A</u>ccept that you have sinned and are in need of a Savior. <u>B</u>elieve that Jesus Christ came and died to save you from your sins. <u>C</u>onfess Him as your Lord and Savior by praying the simple prayer that you have read in this book.

Every one of these stories are true. The names have not been changed to protect the innocent. They did not want it that way. The reason, each one knew they had to deal with their own sin and guilt somehow. They came to the place of desiring a "New Beginning." They each came to the place of accepting the truth when they had a personal encounter with God.

If you need more information or would like to hear more "Real Life Stories" please contact us at Jubilee Worship Center Church of God, 415 North Hobart Road, Hobart, Indiana 46342.

Published By
Jubilee Worship Center
and Step by Step Ministries

Jubilee Worship Center
415 North Hobart Road
Hobart, Indiana 46342
219-947-0301

Step By Step Ministries
215 Sauk Trail
Valparaiso, Indiana 46385
219-762-7589
www.step-by-step.org
www.theshofarman.com

ISBN 0-9676380-9-7

© Copyright 2003 Jubilee Worship Center and Step By Step Ministries

Unless otherwise indicated, all scripture quotations, are taken from the Living Bible © copyright 1988 by Tyndale House Publishers, Inc.